I0189998

Enlightenment's Awakening:
An Onliness Path of Truth-consciousness Realization

Enlightenment's Awakening

An Onliness Path of Truth-consciousness Realization

Transcendence but Inclusion of Pre-egoic, Egoic, and Conditioned Social-Cultural Compound Self Realities

Martin Treon

Auroral Skies Press
Goodyear, Arizona USA
2015

Auroral Skies Press
13348 S. 176th Lane
Goodyear, Arizona 85338
2015

Copyright   2015 by Martin Treon
Cover design by Martin Treon

Library of Congress Control Number: 2014919085
ISBN: Soft cover
0-9655740-5-9
1. Consciousness   2. Awakening   3. Enlightenment.

All rights reserved. No part of this book may be reproduced or transmitted in any form or by any means, electronic or mechanical, including photocopying, recording, or by any information storage and retrieval system, without permission in writing from the copyright owner.

This book was printed in the United States of America.

Passage quotations printed by arrangement with The Acorn Press, P.O. Box 3279, Durham, NC 27715-3279

Other book by Martin Treon:

The Tao of Onliness: An I Ching Cosmology - The Awakening Years

Fires of Consciousness: The Tao of Onliness I Ching

Uncreated Timeless Self of Radiant Emptiness: Onliness Consciousness and Commentaries

Enlightenment Dialogues: A Journey of Post-metaphysical Onliness Awakening

"**Questioner**: Just as a child cannot help growing, so does a man (human), compelled by nature, make progress. Why exert oneself? Where is the need of Yoga (an integral spiritual practice)?

Sri Nisargadatta Maharaj: There is progress all the time. Everything contributes to progress. But this is the progress of ignorance. The circles of ignorance may be ever widening, yet it remains a bondage all the same. In due course a Guru appears to teach and inspire us to practice Yoga and a ripening takes place as a result of which the immemorial night of ignorance dissolves before the rising sun of wisdom. But in reality nothing happens. The sun is always there, there is no night to it; the mind blinded by the 'I-am-the-body' idea spins out endlessly its thread of illusion."

-from: *I Am That: Talks with Sri Nisargadatta Maharaj* (p. 102)

"**Question:** How will the mind become quiescent?

Sri Ramana Maharshi: By the inquiry 'Who am I?' The thought 'Who am I?' will destroy all other thoughts, and like the stick used for stirring the burning pyre, it will itself in the end get destroyed. Then, there will arise Self-realization.

Q: How long should inquiry be practiced?

SRM: As long as there are impressions of objects in the mind, so long the inquiry 'Who am I?' is required. As thoughts arise they should be destroyed then and there in the very place of their origin, through inquiry.

Q: What is wisdom-insight?

SRM: Remaining quiet is what is called wisdom-insight. To remain quiet is to resolve the mind in the Self.

Q: What is the relation between desirelessness and wisdom?

SRM: Desirelessness is wisdom. The two are not different; they are the same. Desirelessness is refraining from turning the mind toward any object. Wisdom means the appearance of no object. In other words, not seeking what is other than the Self is detachment or desirelessness; not leaving the Self is wisdom.

Q: What is liberation?

SRM: Inquiring into the nature of one's self that is in bondage, and realizing one's true nature is liberation."

-from: *Who Am I?: The Teaching of Bhagavan Sri Ramana Maharshi*

"All being is one, and to be fully conscious means to be integrated with the consciousness of all, with the universal self and force and action. . . . The plenitude of this consciousness can only be attained by realizing the identity of the individual self with the transcendent Self, the supreme Reality. . . . This realisation demands a turning of the consciousness inward. The ordinary human consciousness is turned outward and sees the surface of things only. It recoils from entering the inner depths which appear dark and where it is afraid of losing itself. Yet the entry into this obscurity, this void, this silence is the only passage to a greater existence."

-**Sri Aurobindo** (from: *The Future Evolution of Man: The Divine Life upon Earth*)

Contents

To

Noam Chomsky

Chris Hedges

Cornel West

Ralph Nader

Also,

To **Margie**, all my love.

And to our little grandson and granddaughter

Henrik Linus Roe
and
Sylvia Peregrine Roe

May the Winds of Wisdom and Compassion carry You to realms of Beauty, Truth and Goodness.

Preface

This book specifically focuses on the *complete* abandonment and release (transcendence, but inclusion within the context of such transcendence) of predominant-exclusive compound personal-egoic self and consciousness. That is to say, the death of predominant-exclusive pre-egoic, egoic, and conditioned social-cultural compound self. And thus, through this death, there developmentally emerges the *Transformational* subjugation and subsequent integration, the transcendence but inclusion, of compound *personal* egoic self *within* timeless and uncreated *transpersonal* Nondual Self-as-Self Realization, so as to serve and facilitate this Enlightenment Awakened *transcendental* Self Reality.

Thus, by no means of interpretation, and under no circumstances, is the focus and content of this book intended to support or encourage this egocentric and narcissistic predominant-exclusive compound personal-egoic consciousness and self. In this way, this book is neither intended to build up, promote, prolong, soothe, relax, strengthen, enlarge, improve, adjust, or somehow "normalize" this surface compound personal-egoic self, nor is it intended to help one's personal, social-cultural or vocational image, effectiveness or standing, through improvement of the function of this conditional and conditioned compound personal-egoic self. Just the opposite.

Which is to say, if it is this kind of bodymind-focused compound personal-egoic self and consciousness comfort, aid, support, prestige, respite or "normality" that you seek, you *certainly* will not find it here. Rather, you will find this predominant-exclusive superficial compound personal-egoic self and mind consciousness (i.e., relative pre-egoic, egoic, and conditioned social-cultural compound self reality) confronted, exposed, revealed, monitored, abandoned, subjugated, rejected, refused, released and let go of, and thus transformed and transcended, moment-to-moment, at *every* opportunity and turn.

Initially, please understand that the *fundamental* origin and source of One's Comprehension, Recognition and Realization of transcendent Nondual Self-as-Self Enlightenment Consciousness does not arise *from* (is neither *founded* or *centered* within, nor does it *derive* from) pre-egoic, egoic and conditioned social-cultural bodymind oriented compound personal-egoic self realities of mind and consciousness. Rather than being the Origin and Ground of such transcendent Self Awakening and Realization, these relative and conditional pre-personal, personal-egoic, and conditioned social-cultural compound personal-self realities function, *at best*, as the *vehicles* and *vessels-of-conveyance* (the embodied agency and transient means-whereby), *through* (but *not* from) which transcendent Nondual Spirit-as-Spirit Consciousness Self Awakening and Realization occurs. From the onset, understand that You are *not* your body and You are not your mind.

Thus, the *underlying* purpose and premise of this book is *not* at all *centrally* concerned with compound personal-egoic self-involvement, self-importance, self-advancement, self-adulation or self-idolization. Its *central* focus is not about the hubris of personal-ego self's obsessive narcissistic aggrandizement. However, this book is *certainly* concerned with social-cultural, economic and political compound personal-egoic self wellbeing, justice, and equity, which functions to benefit *all* human Beings. Indeed, it is *fundamentally* concerned with world-centric and spiritually-based transcendent Compassion and Loving Kindness toward *all* earth-centered Consciousness Beings and Entities. Thus, I encourage and support individual and group participation and action in *compassionate* and *righteous* social causes, toward social-cultural, economic and political compound personal-egoic self wellbeing, equity, inclusion, and justice, through *democratically based* and *nonviolent* social-political participation, petition, street protest, and civil disobedience, as necessary. In my view, where and when there exists social-cultural, economic or political personal *injustice* and *inequity,* it is necessary that this be directly, straightforwardly, boldly and nonviolently confronted, and *completely* dismantled.

I, as compound personal-egoic self, have been socially-politically active in this way, especially in my early adult life, through a variety of actions, including signing petitions, protest marches, leafleting at supermarkets, using our home as a meeting place for local United Farm Worker Union planning, and faculty-sponsoring a leader of this UFW Union to publicly speak on my campus at Cal State University-Fullerton. I have also participated, through speaking to students and posting information as a faculty member, both in and outside of classes, at Cal State Fullerton (and also speaking as an American Federation of Teachers Union member and vice-president of our Union Local at Cal State Fullerton), and later, speaking in and outside of classes as a faculty member at Washington State University, concerning Cesar Chavez, the UFW Union's efforts and struggles, and about the Grape Boycott itself.

Also, I went door to door collecting donated canned foods near our home in Irvine California, and then driving these up to the UFW Union's center in Delano California for the UFW strikers and their families. I did this together with my then wife, Sharon, who greatly and actively aided and supported me throughout all of these UFW Union volunteer efforts. In this way, I played a *very* minor and limited *local* role in the United Farm Worker's Grape Boycott Movement, led by Cesar Chavez, the late 1960s and early 1970s anti-Viet Nam War demonstration protests, and, some years later, in petitioning and protesting (although not as vigorously as I should have) against the First Gulf War, the Iraq War and Afghanistan War.

First, let me put forward some of the social-cultural-political actions and principles, and sometime practices, that I respect and admire in relation to this U. S. nation-state. For example, this nation-state is a very open and diverse culture-society, with *relative* freedom of written and spoken speech, as well as its provisions for freedom and protection of the press (i.e., one's ability, most often, to speak and write relatively openly and directly concerning social, cultural, economic and political issues). I also respect the *relative* freedom of mobility to travel and reside in differing locations within this country. I especially respect and admire the quality of its many higher education private and public universities and colleges; its provisions and concerns for handicapped and disabled individuals which have emerged especially over the past 40 years; the provisions of its social security programs for the financial security of its elderly retired (and handicapped) individuals; and the widening, but still too limited, opportunities and freedom that women have fought for, and now partially have, emerging especially over the past 40 years or so.

I particularly appreciate the substantial progress in civil rights made by and for African-Americans and Hispanic peoples in the United States (compared to its *savage* and *dismal* state of affairs in the 1950s and before) toward greater social-economic-political equity and justice, although *much* remains to be done in this area. Racism, with its degrading and destructive effects, is still *very much* the deeply rooted feature of this U. S society and culture. In recent history, these gains were primarily initiated and sustained by the nonviolent civil rights movements of the 1960s, led by Martin Luther King Jr., as well as by the nonviolent struggles for economic and working-condition justice, through the grape boycott and related strikes by the United Farm Workers in California, led by Cesar Chavez. Indeed, these two remarkable social-cultural-political leaders, Martin Luther King Jr. and Cesar Chavez, in their unwavering commitment to *nonviolent* truth-force, are, in my view, the modern *founders* for the *peoples* United States nation-state; they are, I would contend, even *more* historically significant and fundamental in this regard, than the group of so-called "founding fathers" of the United States of 1776.

Finally, in relation to the grassroots establishment of a democracy-base worker-centered and worker owned and operated economy, I'm encouraged by the moderate, but gradually increasing, involvement of people in community based cooperatives of all sorts (e.g., credit unions, food cooperatives, farmer's markets, communal vegetable gardens, cooperative child daycare), as well as by the cooperative community-based establishment and ownership of affordable housing, water and energy utilities. I'm *especially* encouraged with the gradual growth of interest in, and establishment of, worker or employee owned, controlled and managed businesses and companies. If such a democratized workplace were to emerge as the predominant standard and norm for those who work, such pervasive worker ownership and control of their own businesses and companies would, I believe, result in an greatly increased *diversity of capital ownership* (wealth) within and across the whole workforce population of the United States, as Gar Alperovitz, Richard Wolff, Chris Hedges, Ralph Nader and Noam Chomsky have variously discussed.

In matters and issues of social-cultural, economic and political policy and action, as well as in relation to the news and historical record, I do *not* look to the *corporately controlled* mainstream U. S. media for in-depth, objective and truthful information and understanding. Rather, I turn for this to the writings, and also to visual social media interviews and presentations (on internet sites like YouTube.com, truthdig.com, democracynow.org, for example), of social commentators and critics like Chris Hedges, Noam Chomsky, Ralph Nader, Bill Moyers, Cornel West, Michael Moore, Glenn Greenwald, Richard D. Wolff, Gar Alperovitz, Steve Fraser, Matt Tabbi, Naomi Klein, Jim Hightower, Mary Christina Wood, Jeremy Scahill, Howard Zinn, Amy Goodman, Jill Stein, Edward Said, Margaret Flowers, Henry Giroux, Morris Berman, Rania Masri, Peter Dreier, Lawrence Lessig, Heidi Boghosian, Mike Lofgren, and others.

Historically, and currently, it is *primarily* this corrupt and anti-democratic unregulated *corporate roulette-style* and *business-money obsessed* terminal form of capitalism that *controls* (primarily through its massive infusion of campaign money to people running for political office) the social, political and economic directions and policies of the United States government. Terminal, because it is fundamentally based on escalating egoic-based human *acquisition-possession, avarice, fear* and *greed*, and thus, I would assert, it ultimately devolves, self-consumes, and self-implodes, so as to terminate itself through its own circular, self-directed actions (based on such blind self-feeding and ever-expanding acquisition-possession, avarice, fear and greed). This self-destructive system especially prevails in the United States.

In my view, capitalism, in general, founded and sustained as it is on acquisition-possession, avarice, greed and fear in *all* of its systemic forms, is ethically and morally an *inherently* destructive, unjust and inhumane social-cultural, political and economic way of life. In my view, the exploitative and profit-driven-at-all-costs fundamental *inherency* of capitalism, as a way of economic life, is a functional manifestation and expression of the current developmental-evolutionary level of earth-centered human consciousness realization. And thus, I would assert that capitalism will not be *fundamentally* transcended toward a more truly constructive, just and humane way of economic life, unless and until there occurs, on a larger-scale, a more transcendentally Consciousness-inclusive Wisdom and Compassion Awakening and Realization in human development-evolution. However, *if* and *until* there emerges such a potential transcendental Consciousness Transformation of greater Loving Kindness and Truthfulness toward *all* Consciousness Being and Entities, this does *not* mean that *limited,* but critical and important, improvements toward a more constructive, just, equitable and humane social-cultural, political and economic way of life cannot be accomplished.

Predominantly, in my view, the United States government has devolved into, and now functions as, a security-and-surveillance state, operated almost exclusively to protect and sustain the world-wide interests and financial wealth of corporations and the wealthiest of individuals. That is to say, by specifically supporting and sustaining the richest one or two percent of its whole population, while either primarily ignoring, or actively working in basic opposition to, the interests, concerns, and welfare of the remaining 98 to 99 per cent of its population. Currently in the United States, there exists a *corrupt,* money manipulated and controlled, corporate-welfare state-supported form of anti-democratic totalitarian-based capitalism, that now *pervasively* dominates and *effectively* controls the major political-governmental and financial levers of influence and power, with resultant obscenely greater and greater financial income disparity between this tiny percentage of the population versus the vast majority of people.

In *conjunction with* this pervasive corporate-capitalism economic and political domination problem, is the existence in the United States of a culture that (partly because of the frustration, despair and resignation of many if not most of its people) strongly tends toward violence and soulless material acquisition-possession. In regard to this U.S. cultural tendency toward violence (and its obsession with guns), not surprisingly, there additionally exists a culture of perpetual-war mentality, with a resultant endless sequence of wars fought and subsequent ongoing selections of new-found enemies. This culturally, economically, and historically based perpetual war mentality is supported by an ever-expanding, dominating, occupying, and bullying militarily-based *world-imperial empire* pathway that the United States has taken, with thousands of U. S. troops stationed in numerous U. S. bases within the borders of other nation-states, all around the world.

Recently, the U. S government has implemented a truly Orwellian program of *total surveillance* and digital recording and storage of *all* telephone, computer email and social media communications and messaging of each and every citizen in the United States. This is now an established reality, implemented through the long arm of its National Security Administration (in collusion with the FBI and with CIA cooperation and support). This massive electronic monitoring and storage is an all-out invasion of the privacy and the private personal communications of *each* and *every* citizen, and is rationalized under the *fear mongering* guise of "national security." Imagine the hesitancy and sense of cautiousness that this pervasive governmental surveillance now engenders in individuals who wish to expression their objections to and criticisms of U. S. national policies, plans, programs and actions. Consider the damper of self-censoring that such surveillance will tend to produce in all citizens.

Under these conditions, citizens will tend to be fearful and "think twice" about critically speaking their minds concerning this government and its proclamations and questionable activities. So much for freedom of speech and expression. Using this destructive U. S government surveillance pathway, *all* of your private and personal records of interaction and communication with other people can, at any time, be dragged up (and even edited by the government if necessary) and used against you. That is, used to punish, detain and isolated you, if they don't like your comments and criticisms of their policies and programs. This is a new low in monitoring, and thus suppression, of personal and open speech and written communication by the U. S government.

To further complicate and intensify these *destructive* pathway problems, is the predominantly nation-state-centric and often politically passive, indifferent, compliant, ego-self-interest absorbed, easily redirected-distracted, superficially entertained, celebrity-oriented, consumerism fixated and business money-hustling *obsessed* ethos and mentality of many, is not most, of the people, *not excluding myself*, in the United States. An example of this population's indifference, superficiality, egocentric self-interest absorption, and passive inaction is its unwillingness to demand and initiate *immediate* and *decisive* social-economic-political action to *radically* eliminate human-generated environmental greenhouse gas pollution in the United States, so as to substantially contribute to the avoidance of approaching world-wide temperature increases, and the resultant horrific and tragic human and environmental consequences of such world-wide climate change.

Although quite often politically apathetic (consider the relatively low percentage in the U. S. population that even bothers to vote in major elections), I would add, however, that the people of the United States themselves, in the course of their everyday lives, are, in my experience, generally hard working, productive, practical, inventive-creative, reasonably intelligent, independent, honest and generous individuals. These are people who do the best they can under difficult social-cultural, economic and political existing circumstances. Note also, that an important factor in the U. S. population's low voter-election turnout apathy is due to the fact, as Noam Chomsky has rightly pointed out, that there is really only *one party* to vote for in the United States, the corporately controlled "Business Party," with its two Democratic Party and Republican Party branches. And there exists only *very* minor and relatively trivial social-political-economic differences between these two branches - not socially-culturally, economically and politically *real, substantial* and *contrasting* difference, and thus not an *authentic* choice, between them. That is, the "choice" is between tweedle-dee and tweedle-dum. In short, the continuing pursuit of these destructive and deeply embedded social-cultural, economic and political *pathologic* pathways noted above will, in my view, *certainly not* in any way enable or permit this nation-state to *survive* as such, for any extended period of historic time.

Put otherwise, this militaristic and totalitarian-oriented corporate-capitalist based American Imperialistic Empire is in the process of social-cultural, economic and political self destruction and death; it is currently and rapidly historically dying. Of course, I cling to the fond and precarious hope, and strongly *prefer* and *support* the slim possibility, that this dying Imperialist Empire nation-state is replaced by a *much* more socially-culturally, economically and politically equitable, just, peaceful, compassionate and wise *world-centric* and *truly democratic* society and culture.

The *profound* and *extensive* consequent human suffering, misery and agony that would derive from the social-economic-political United States implosion and collapse would, of course, socially-culturally and personally devastate the people in the United States, but would also cause great turmoil, suffering and misery for *all* people, all around the world. One could speculate that, in theory, it may be possible for the people of the United States to nonviolently *completely* uproot and abandon these social-cultural, economic and political pathologic pathways, but without individuals (on a large human scale) *first* developing-evolving toward a more profound *Transformation* of personal and transpersonal Consciousness Awakening, such a *complete* and *nonviolent* uprooting and abandonment is, in my view, not a very realistic possibility.

Thus, given the *current* realm-wave *level* of human developmental-evolutionary personal, transpersonal, social, and ethical-moral Consciousness, the likelihood that a more *authentically* democratic, world-centric, socially-culturally, economically and politically equitable, nonviolent, peaceful, open, compassionate, and thoughtful-mindful community might *possibly* replace such a United States social-economic-political implosion and collapse is, I think, *very* improbable. Indeed, as others have also pointed out, if such an implosion and collapse does occur, the *real* possibility of an *extreme* socially-culturally, economically and politically inequitable, repressive, authoritarian, and aggressive oligarchic governing plutocracy future for the United States is not at all unlikely.

I strongly suspect that Chris Hedges is correct in his view that, given the current dysfunctional state of affairs at this critical juncture in United States and world history, the *only* option that the majority of people in the United States have left, so as to turn back and avoid the likely future of a socially, economically and politically repressive, authoritarian and undemocratic (i.e., toxic) governing oligarchic plutocracy, involves direct, sustained and intense *nonviolent* resistance, rebellion and revolt (e.g., strikes, boycotts, civil disobedience, street protests) by *large* numbers of people. This will involve *organized* and *concretely content focused* individual and group *nonviolent* (in relation to both people and property) resistance, protest, defiance, obstruction, and civil disobedience (i.e., active nonviolent resistance and revolution). As Hedges correctly points out, this may well fail (under present circumstances I would say, indeed, this is quite likely to fail), but, despite such very possible failure, we have to at least *try* this last remaining route of redress, for our children's and grandchildren's sake if for no other reason.

However, *beyond* failing or succeeding in this endeavor (beyond the American Empire's cultural obsession with "winning" and "losing"), the more *profound* and *central* reason for the necessity of such active nonviolent resistance, protest and revolt, given these multiple pathologic pathways, is that this is *righteous* and *just* action. That is to say, righteous and just in that such nonviolent action is taken to facilitate the establishment of a more world-centric, democratic, humane, ecologically balanced and sustainable, peaceful, open, equitable, just and nonviolent social-economic-political existence for all human beings. Such action, in turn, would also have *profound* implications for human beings world-wide, and thus also for the ecology of the whole living earth itself.

Speaking optimistically then, the implications for the establishment of such a more just, equitable, democratic, and humane social-economic-political environment would, as suggested, not only be limited to the people of United States society-culture, but would also profoundly and constructively influence and affect all peoples and cultures, all around the world. But under *no* circumstance *whatsoever* can such active *nonviolent* resistance, protest and revolt be allowed to devolve into violence *of any sort,* on the part of those who protest. Such violence would, I believe, *certainly* doom such a United States people's revolution to utter and tragic failure.

The public and private colleges and universities of the United States (and indeed of the world for that matter) are certainly one of the great intellectual-social-cultural accomplishments, the central learning and teaching "Crown Jewels," of this culture and society. Over a period of fifty years, I've had an up-close and personal knowledge and experience in relation to several of these important institutions. Starting as a college freshman at the University of Minnesota-Minneapolis in 1955, and then going on to graduate school at Stanford University and then UCLA, to my retirement fifty years later as a tenured full professor in Communication Sciences and Disorders at Texas A&M University-Kingsville in 2005, I've witnessed the broad evolutionary patterns these institutions of higher learning in the United States have taken over these years.

I was a university student for nine of these 50 years, and a university faculty member, ascending through the academic ranks from instructor to tenured full professor, for 28 of these 50 years (37 of these 50 years in academia overall). I taught and did research as a faculty member at public universities in the western United States (in California and Washington), in the Midwest (in Chicago Illinois), in the east (in Plattsburgh New York), in the south (in south Texas and New Mexico), and in the north (in South Dakota). The evolutionary trends that I *directly* observed in all of these U. S.

public universities over this period, which were basically the same trends that were occurring in almost all public colleges and universities nation-wide as best I could determine, amounted to a short-sighted and devastating virtual abandonment by the majority of the people in this country of the financial (tax-base), and thus the social-cultural, *support* needed for the low-tuition functioning of these public universities and colleges. And these ongoing abandonment trends were approved and accomplished by the very public *themselves* who *own* and have *direct responsibility for* these institutions of higher learning, and are supposed (required) to maintain and develop them. How sad and tragic.

I witnessed over these 50 years, an absent sense of *sacrifice* and senseless *short-sightedness* of the majority of this U. S. population, that expressed itself through their refusal to pay the necessary and sufficient ongoing tax revenues so as to *fully* fund their *own* public universities and colleges, so that *every* academically qualified student could *easily* afford to attend them at *both* the undergraduate and graduate school levels *without* going into any debt whatsoever (i.e., with very minimal or *no* student tuition). Instead, this population has shifted (dumped) far too much of this public financial responsibility onto: (1) its own and its future college student children, in the form of absurdly inflated and unaffordable tuition costs (partly caused by excessive and expensive expenditures by the colleges and universities themselves, on spa-like recreational student facilities which do not in the least relate or contribute to academic and scholarly teaching-learning quality and depth) with resultant devastating student and student family loans and debt, and (2) the corrupt exploit-commodify-and-monetize *everything* for profit *mentality* of private capitalist corporations, so that they can *vocationally* recruit and train their future employees in the ways of their corruption. And, in so doing, they distort and trivialize our young people's intellectual life of higher learning and development. In this process, the whole culture's money-obsessed and corporate-capitalist-oriented societal influences have functioned to significantly convert these institutions of higher learning into banal corporate-business based *vocational training* centers, in which such potential reason and critical-thinking based scholarly institutions are now operated and function, *as if* they were themselves *consumer-based* corporate businesses.

In this *distorted* consumer-commercial context, academic faculty are substantially evaluated and judged for promotion and retention *not* primarily based on their *actual* scholarly teaching and research accomplishments (i.e., by the *specific* content and potential of their academic and intellectual scholarly efforts, achievements, insights, creativity and contributions), but rather by the explicit disclosure and touting of how many financial grants and how much *money* they have acquired to *fund* their research *and* to fill the university coffers. Such money-oriented grant disclosure is *not* at all a *true* and *direct* measure and indication of an academic faculty person's *actual* imaginative, insightful, original and creative intellectual and scholarly accomplishments and contributions. Getting grant money to enable you to do your research is *not* an *academic* or *scholarly* accomplishment and achievement, any more than breathing, eating, or getting enough sleep to enable you to do your research are academic or scholarly accomplishments and achievements.

In my experience, it is substantially and unfortunately true that, as Noam Chomsky and Cornell West have both pointed out, the great *majority* of teaching and learning occurring at these college and university centers of higher learning tends to be focused on issues of social-cultural *indoctrination, memorization, conformity and obedience* oriented content, not excluding much of my own teaching. Nonetheless, there are still some creative, insightful, innovative, and challenging liberal arts and sciences faculty, and students within these colleges and universities, who courageously speak to (teach and learn) the more widely ignored, denied and unpopular *reality* of social-economic-political-environmental conditions and circumstances (i.e., who dare to speak truth to power). But, overall, it is as if the *central* purpose for a college's or university's existence, and a student's *primary* reason and focus for attending a college or university, has devolved into a teaching-learning experience of indoctrination into, conformity with, and obedience to this society's particular social-economic-political money-oriented practices, values and perspectives, with special emphasis upon the intellectually narrow focus of finding and teaching-learning a vocation-profession, so as to get a job and make money.

Also, there has occurred a self-indulgent and unrealistic United States *societal value* change over these years that suggests that *everyone* should be able to go to college-university, rather than recognizing that such high levels of learning and teaching are appropriate *only* for those students who have, and can somehow demonstrate, the potential academic-cognitive talents and abilities to function *at* these levels. First and foremost, for undergraduate and graduate college and university students, the liberal arts, literature and the humanities need to take center stage in their study and learning. Within this context, it is my view that the underlying and overriding *central purpose* and *critical function* of each and every authentic college and university must be *unwaveringly* focused on each student's open-ended and broadly-based *intellectual awakening, realization* and *enlightenment*, in relation to the use of critical reasoning, as well as challenge to and critic of, *all* knowledge, insight and understanding, controversial and otherwise.

Thus, the *primary* purpose, function and central goal of authentic colleges and universities *cannot at all* be merely the *indoctrination* into, and *information training* of, students, so as to subsequently fill the work-vocational job-slots of the business community's state subsidized and undemocratically oriented corporate-capitalist fear-and-greed-based economy. But, of course, *all* people*, tuition free*, should be able to pursue their interests and talents, whatever they may be, through varied and diverse educational schooling opportunities, for as long as they wish and to whatever level they can achieve.

Together, all of the distorted and primarily destructive pathway changes within these U. S. institutions of higher learning, which I've observed and experienced over this 50 year period (nine years as a student and 28 years as a faculty member), has, in my view, had this result: (1) the meaning and substance of "academic freedom," within academia, has now become a joke, in the sense that deeply rooted, *profound* and *controversial* content issues and conflicts are carefully avoided, evaded, suppressed or ignored, and radically creative and controversial faculty are not retained, and (2) universities and colleges have, more and more, become glorified vocational, technical, and corporate business-oriented schools, *rather than* great centers of intellectual awakening, creativity, excitement and controversy, which include in-depth and broad-spectrum exposure to, and debate of, humanity's universal concerns, issues, knowledge and wisdom in the sciences, arts, humanities, philosophy and literature.

Reference to the role of the *I Ching* (The Book of Change) comes up in my discussion of its important contribution to the conceptual formulation of Onliness theory and perspective, and thus I wish to initially comment on it. As discussed in all of my books, the *I Ching* and its Onliness addendum, the *Tao of Onliness I Ching*, are *not* "magic" fortune-teller games. From Onliness theory and perspective, *mindful* consultation of the *I* Ching is considered an *early-stage* forms of meditation-contemplation, *toward* transcendental Awakening and Realization. From Onliness perspective, then, one uses the *I Ching,* and *Tao of Onliness I Ching* supplement, as a *vehicle* in this way; as a *mindful* and *intuitive* opportunity One has to *inwardly* view both compound personal-egoic self and transpersonal Self, primarily through advanced vision-logic consciousness eyes.

However, note here philosopher Ken Wilber's warnings concerning his "pre-personal/trans-personal fallacy" conception (i.e., the confounding and mistaking of pre-personal for trans-personal awareness and experience or, conversely, the confusing of trans-personal for pre-personal Awareness and Experience); especially, in this case, when consulting the *I Ching* and *Tao of Onliness I Ching* for, and in relation to, *transcendental* transpersonal Consciousness (not compound personal-egoic self of consciousness) meditative purposes. This confounding tends to occur because *I Ching* has historically so often been seen, used, and interpreted in magic or mythic "fortune-teller" terms.

Used in a mindful and meditative way for *transpersonal* consultation purposes, the *I Ching* and *Tao of Onliness I Ching* are simply means of *facilitating* one's *intuitive insight* into one's own Consciousness. There is nothing "magical" or "mysterious" about it.

In this way, as Wilber says, one must carefully guard against and avoid confusing and confounding *pre-rational* and *pre-personal* levels of human developmental-evolutionary awareness (e.g., archaic, magic, mythic levels of consciousness) with transcendent *trans-rational* and *trans-personal* levels of Consciousness; that is, of misinterpreting and mistaking the former for the latter, or the latter for the former, with disastrous results.

In this way, the central purpose of *Tao of Onliness I Ching* meditation-contemplation is to provide an *initial* (early-stage) way toward *Intuitive* transpersonal Awakening to Our own true *transcendental* Nature, Identity and Condition. That is, through opening Our eyes, if only fleetingly, to Our always, already fully Enlightened Buddha-nature and Christ-consciousness. Ultimately, such *Awakening* involves the transformation and conversion of anger, hate, greed, possessiveness, fear, indifference, cruelty, aversion, self-contraction, ego-centrism, self-importance, ignorance and delusion into Compassion, Wisdom, Insight, Uncontracted Openness, Truthfulness, Equanimity, Courage, Forgiveness, Patience, Loving Kindness, and Generosity. That is to say, toward *Expressions* of transcendent *Nondual Self-as-Self* Consciousness Realization.

Ultimately, Awakening to Spirit, to Self, (i.e., the *transcendent* Ascent of Spirit in Wisdom) is *inseparable* from the direct and committed Compassionate application and practice of such Awakening in relation to all manifest Consciousness Beings and Entities (i.e., the *immanent* Descent of Spirit in Compassion). Note however, that such Awakening to transcendent Nondual Self, to *Absolute Reality*, ultimately cannot occur through mental thought and knowledge alone, no matter how refined or extensive. Rather, it occurs *only* through One's *direct* transcendental Experience and Awareness. Such Ascending-Descending Awakening to One's transpersonal Self Nature and Condition is ultimately *not,* of Itself, *mental* but *trans-mental*, not of Itself pre-personal (pre-egoic) or personal (egoic), but *trans-personal* (trans-egoic), and not of Itself pre-rational or rational, but *trans-rational*.

I fully accept and embrace the manifest Form *flux* and

impermanence of *all* phenomenal manifestation, and that, *in Truth*, no separate and exclusive *individual* compound personal-egoic self exists, and that *pain* is inherent in manifest Form embodiment, and finally, that *all* Beings are always, already *fully* Enlightened and have full and immediate access to *Realization* of this Enlightenment Reality, but very often do not Realize such Enlightenment Consciousness because of pre-personal-pre-egoic, personal-egoic, and conditioned social-cultural compound self reality's mind of blindness, ignorance and delusion.

May the merit of my presentation of the content of this book benefit *all* Beings and Consciousness, in all Worlds and Universes inclusive, toward the *cessation* of each One's suffering this day, and toward the *Realization* by Each this day, of Our inherent, already fully Enlightened Buddha-nature. Homage to the Buddha, homage to the Dharma, homage to the Sangha. Please understand that the content of this paragraph derives from the spiritual tradition of *non-theistic* Zen Buddhism, which of course, in turn, derives from the broader spiritual tradition of *non-theistic* Buddhism itself.

Pre-personal-Pre-egoic, Personal-Egoic, and Conditioned Social-Cultural Compound Self Identity Transcendence but Inclusion

"His heart is with Brahman
His eyes in all things
Sees only Brahman
Equally present,
Knows his own Atman
In every creature
And all creation
Within that Atman."

-from: *The Bhagavad-Gita* (translated by Swami Prabhavananda and Christopher Isherwood)

"**Questioner:** Sir, I am a humble seeker, wandering from Guru to Guru in search of release. My mind is sick, burning with desire, frozen with fear. My days flit by, red with pain, grey with boredom. . . . At this rate I shall live in sorrow and die in despair. Is there any hope for me?

Sri Nisargadatta Maharaj: Nothing is wrong with you, but the ideas you have of yourself are altogether wrong. It is not you who desires, fears and suffers, it is the person built on the foundation of your body by circumstances and influences. You are not that person. This must be clearly established in your mind and never lost sight of. . . . You are the Supreme Reality beyond the world and its creator, beyond consciousness and its witness, beyond all assertions and denials. Remember it, think on it, act on it. Abandon all sense of separation, see yourself in all and act accordingly. With action bliss will come and, with bliss, conviction. . . . Once you began to experience the peace, love and happiness which need no outer causes, all your doubts will dissolve. Just catch hold of what I told you and live by it."

-from: *I Am That: Talks with Sri Nisargadatta Maharaj* (pp. 369-370)

Supreme Self has No Qualities Whatsoever, and has All Qualities Whatsoever

You see, there's really *nothing* to say. In Truth, there's nothing that needs to be said, but, mostly unnecessarily, I'll say it anyway. First, understand that *All* is Spirit, *All* is Self, there *is* no other Than. In Truth, this transcendent *Self* You are has *no qualities* whatsoever, is unqualifable, and at once is and has *all qualities* whatsoever, and yet *is* neither of these at all. This *perfect* Emptiness that is *so* Full, this Bliss and Freedom. Do not be fearful, downhearted or discouraged. *As* this *Divine* and *Sacred* transcendent Self You already are, have *always* been and will *ever* be, You need not fear or be afraid. There is nothing to be lost, desired, or gained; there is no winning or losing to occur. Surrender to, and Rest Silently within, this Luminous *Omnipresent Self* You are. Indeed, such *Silence* and *Surrender* is the Way of Self Awakening. Do not hold back or withdraw from this *Supreme Surrender*. Simply *Be* who You truly *are*. And in this Way Realize and Embrace this *timeless*, *all-inclusive* and *uncreated* Self You already are.

I wonder if You doubt what I've just said to You? Do not. These words I speak to You are True. Test them for Yourself, through physical body, emotion, mind, World Soul, and Spirit centered mindful and ongoing practice and meditation. Look *deeply* into this Awakened *Nondual* Self-as-Self You are, which is *All* and *None*, Every-thing and No-thing. See if what I say is True or False; *See* This for Yourself. Indeed, it is *only* through Your own direct, immediate, and unmediated *transcendental* Experience and Awareness that You will *ever* truly See and Know this *Supreme Reality* of Self, which I speak of in My Teachings here.

From the onset, understand that You are *not* your relative and conditional bodymind self. *Obsessive* compound pre-egoic, egoic, and conditioned social-cultural consciousness (i.e., predominant-exclusive *bodymind* compound personal-egoic self identity) effectively *precludes* such transcendent Awakening, and maintains this limited and conditional consciousness of *small mind* in its worldspace of ignorance, delusion and suffering. This small mind of self-contracted and self-sustaining blind and circular consciousness is the relative pre-transcendental consciousness mind of compound personal-egoic self and consciousness (as opposed to transcendental Mind, big Mind, of Nondual Self and Consciousness Awakening). It is within small mind's consciousness that there appears to be *no* option to this conditioned and conditional predominant-exclusive compound personal-egoic self reality, not even an *awareness* of possible exit or transcendence.

This is the fear-filled, grasping and searching *mind* of separate-self-sense *pre-egoic, egoic* and *conditioned social-cultural* compound personal-egoic self, this separate and isolated worldspace consciousness of birth and death. And the strange thing is, that most humans appear to believe that this self of mind is the *only* worldspace consciousness possible within earthly human life existence. That *this* life of predominant-exclusive pre-egoic, egoic and conditioned social-cultural bodymind identity and consciousness is the *only* one available to we earth-centered human beings. But this simply is *not* True. Indeed, it's very far from True.

However, it is not that predominant-exclusive compound personal-egoic consciousness is "bad" and that inclusive trans-egoic Consciousness is "good." The *protection, development* and *unveiling* of compound personal-ego self and consciousness toward personal-egoic wisdom and maturity is critically important to the wellbeing of personal-egoic separate-self-sense bodymind. Effective compound personal-ego consciousness *importantly* functions to monitor, integrate, and coordinate the many and varied dimensions of the bodymind's compound personal-egoic self reality, within this *personal* temporal world of birth and death. But to Realize higher transcendent, *transpersonal* realm-waves of Consciousness, predominant-exclusive identification with and as pre-egoic, egoic and conditioned social-cultural compound self of mind *must* be negated and preserved, must be *transcended,* but *included* within the context of such higher Consciousness transcendence. Ultimately then, You must die to predominant-exclusive compound personal-ego consciousness self identity; there must occur the effective *death* of separate-self-sense pre-egoic, egoic and conditioned social-cultural compound self and consciousness.

My Teachings are Radical, Demanding and Transformative

The way I Teach is *radical* and *demanding*. My Teachings are not easy, soft, or quick-fix in nature. Rather, they're difficult, challenging, transformative, and often personally very disruptive. They will *not* protect, comfort, soothe or bolster your predominant-exclusive compound personal-egoic *illusionary* separate-self-sense bodymind consciousness identity. My Teachings tend to be *direct* and *blunt*, and do *not* take or shift responsibility from You. You are the target of My Teachings; it is *at You* that I take uncompromising Aim. It is *with You* that I openly and directly share these Teachings. First, from the beginning, and by way of *fundamental* orientation, look to the *Tao Te Ching*; understand, cultivate and practice the *Tao,* so as to respond to and resonate with this *Way* of the *Watercourse.*

As Your teacher and guide, come to and learn from Me and from My Teachings. In Truth, I Am You - *unconditionally, timelessly, completely,* and thus I Am *always* with You. But *also* Understand that Your Realization of Enlightenment Awakening does *not* depend upon Me or My Teachings. You always, already *fully* are this Bliss-Divine Awakened Nondual Self Reality, this *unspeakable* Reality and Consciousness of *Truth.* Indeed, You must come to *utterly transcend*, while yet *including* from the Consciousness of such transcendence, Me and My Teachings. This is My *first* and *final* Teaching to You.

I speak with You here and now from the realm-wave of advanced *vision-logic* worldspace consciousness. Within and from this worldspace, the *most* that conventional language can do is to suggestively point and metaphorically intimate the deep nature and meaning of Awakening to Enlightenment. Such *direct* Realization Itself is *far* beyond the compound personal-egoic consciousness based convention of language communication and meaning. But, of course, with You now, I must *use* conventional language to *indirectly* point to and metaphorically imply the deep transpersonal, trans-egoic meaning of *Nondual Self* Recognition and Realization Consciousness.

Such Realization is *trans-egoic,* in the sense that Self of Nondual Consciousness *transcends* but *includes,* negates and preserves, compound personal-egoic self reality and consciousness. That is, compound pre-egoic, personal-egoic and conditioned social-cultural relative self, and its consciousness of small mind, is *transcended* yet preserved, in that it no longer *predominantly-exclusively* serves one's egocentric narcissistic compound personal-egoic self. Rather, it is now integrated into, thus included within, this *causeless, infinite* and *all-inclusive* Nondual Self Reality Consciousness that You *truly* are, have *ever* been and will *always* be. In this way, compound pre-egoic, egoic and conditioned social-cultural self of pre-transcendental consciousness awareness can now *facilitate* and *serve* One's transcendental Consciousness *Realization* of Nondual Self-as-Self Awakening.

You are Bliss-Divine Self of All and None, Each and Every, Only and Completely

This uncreated, timeless *Self* of Radiant Emptiness is Your *True* Nature and Condition, is Your Supreme Bliss-Divine Identity and Home. Do not be afraid of or turn away from this *Ultimate Reality* of transcendent Mind that You always already are, even *here* and *now.* There is nothing to fear and, in Fact, there is no *Authentic Way* in which You *can* turn from this Reality, that in *Truth* You are. There is neither a Way to turn *from,* nor a Place to turn *to,* which is not this transcendent Nondual Self-as-Self Reality and Consciousness that You always already are. Beloved, as Bliss-Divine Self You are *All* and *None, Each* and *Every, Only* and *Completely.* But understand, this is certainly *not* True of you as interactive and predominant-exclusive pre-egoic, personal-egoic, and conditioned social-cultural compound self identity of *relative* reality and consciousness.

In ever-changing and ever-evolving *impermanent* manifest Form Reality, there is *only* change, *only* impermanence. *Embrace* this impermanence. This *personal* human embodiment of Self, which You have now assumed, is indeed one of ever-evolving impermanence and change; it is the *manifest Form* of One's earth-centered human life of birth and death. And *inherent* to such manifest human embodiment is its joy and pain, growth, development and decay, happiness and sorrow, birth, injury, disease and death. There is *nothing* to fear about, nor is there cause to self-contract from, this ever-changing embodiment that You've assumed. Rather, *embrace* and *welcome* the great developmental-evolutionary *opportunity* of this manifestation of human bodymind impermanence that You *temporarily* are.

What Specifically is the Way of Onliness Enlightenment Awakening

Onliness is a broadly based developmental-evolutionary Way or Path of Enlightenment, among many other *equally* valid and authentic Ways of Enlightenment Awakening. In Onliness theory, *in addition to* the predominantly predisposing developmental-evolutionary holon-pole and holon-polarity realm-waves that comprise the Enlightenment Realization Mode or Way of *Onliness*, I've put forward seven *other* predominantly predisposing Enlightenment Realization Modes: Am, Actlessness, Radiance, Emptiness, Awakening, Mystery, and Mind (see Figures 5 and 7). In relation to the *specific* nature and content of the developmental Consciousness realm-waves of Onliness itself, I have, in my other books, described the particular spiritually *facilitative* transpersonal influences of each of the holon-pole and holon-polarity realm-waves of Onliness Consciousness, which comprise this Enlightenment Realization *Mode*.

Onliness asserts that *each* and *every* Consciousness Being and Entity is *Sacred, Holy* and *Divine*. And that the *highly* varied and diverse Consciousness Beings and Entities that tend to identify with and follow the Way of Onliness, are *predominantly* predisposed to do so as a function of their own natively *inherent* nature and make-up, *interacting with* their acquired developmental environmentally based experiences. Thus, it is *through* a Consciousness Being's or Entity's self-awareness and self-recognition of the nature of their own temperament and predispositions, that certain Beings and Entities *self-selectively* come to identify with and follow the Way of Onliness Awakening.

Onliness, in its initial transcendent Consciousness realm-waves, is fundamentally a Way of yin-and-yang holonic-polarity-within-unity. In this regard, the *I Ching* (The Book of Change), and its extensive consultation, was importantly employed in the polarity-oriented conceptual formulation of Onliness theory and perspective (see my notes on the *I Ching* in the Preface of this book). Also, see Ken Wilber's writings for definitions of the terms "holon" and "holonic," and my own previous writings for definitions of the terms "holon-pole," "holon-polarity," "holon-polar" and "holonic-polaric." Beings who are *predisposed* to follow the Way of Onliness will, within this Path of Onliness, tend toward either the *yin* or the *yang* holon-pole of a holon-polarity realm-wave of Onliness Consciousness (see Figures 5 and 7). *Yang* Onliness Consciousness predominantly tends toward the personal and transpersonal *Experiential* emphasis of *Righteousness* within *Compassion*. *Yin* Onliness Consciousness predominantly tends toward the personal and transpersonal *Awareness* emphasis of *Intuition* within *Knowledge* (see Figure 5 to view these relationships).

But beyond these *singular* holon-pole influences, it is the spiritually facilitative influences toward transcendent Consciousness Awakening of the *interaction* of these holon-poles that are fundamental and primary. For the Mode of Onliness Awakening, these primary *holon-polarities* are: either yin *Intuition-Righteousness* or yang *Righteousness-Intuition*, which, in turn, respectively derive from the holon-polarities of yin *Knowledge-Compassion* or yang *Compassion-Knowledge*, which, in turn, respectively derive from the holon-polarities of yin *Awareness-Experience* or yang *Experience-Awareness*. In this way, these tend to be the *predominantly* predisposing holon-polarities for Consciousness Beings and Entities who follow the *Way* of Onliness (see this visualized in Figure 5). However, You need to understand that Beings and Entities of the Enlightenment Realization Mode of Onliness are also, but to a lesser extent, *variously* influenced by the many *spiritually facilitative* holon-pole and holon-polarity realm-wave tendencies of the other *seven* Enlightenment Awakening Ways or Modes. And this occurs *in addition to* such

Beings' or Entities' above described *predominant* predispositional holon-pole and holon-polarity spiritually facilitative realm-wave tendencies of their *native* Onliness Consciousness.

The Ultimate Meaning and Nature of Onliness is Unfathomable and Unknowable

The Meaning of Onliness Itself is *transpersonal, trans-mental, trans-rational,* and *trans-compound personal-egoic* in nature, and can be Known *only* through Consciousness Awakening within transcendental Experience *and* Awareness. The *deep* Meaning of Onliness is thus Unfathomable and Unknowable in self-contracted compound *personal-egoic* self of consciousness reality. And, in this way, Onliness is *fundamentally* indefinable and indescribable through language meaning and definition, which is the central communicative medium and mode of this relative and conditional consciousness. Thus, in compound personal-egoic self surface consciousness, the Meaning and Nature of Onliness Awakening can only be *superficially* described and understood.

From Onliness perspective, *each* individual Consciousness Being and Entity has Its *unique* Pattern or Way of Enlightenment Awakening and Realization. That is, each such Being and Entity has Its own *original* and *characteristic* combination of dimensions, features, intensities and interactions that facilitate such transcendent Realization. And keep in mind, that a Being or Entity who is predominantly predisposed to the Way of Onliness will *also* always, and to varying degrees and in varied and unique combinations, *include* the spiritually facilitative influences of *all* of the holon-pole and holon polarity realm-wave dimensions that comprise *all* of the other *seven* Enlightenment Modes of Nondual Self-as-Self Consciousness Realization (see Figures 5 and 7).

To better visualize this, look at Figures 3, 5 and 7. As conceptualized in Onliness theory, in *addition* to Onliness itself, the other *seven* Modes or Ways of Enlightenment Realization that emerge in Consciousness, beginning at the realm-wave level of Subtle Prim-istence, include yin and yang: Mind, Mystery, Awakening, Emptiness, Radiance, Actlessness, and Am. But understand that these eight realm-wave Modes of Enlightenment could *just as well*, in other conceptual or social-cultural terms and contexts, be alternatively and correctly defined and described in *other* Ways; or, indeed, they could be divided into *any number*, even a nearly infinite number, of *Modes* or *Ways* of transcendent Consciousness Awakening and Realization.

Searching for, Seeking and Achieving Enlightenment Consciousness

To strive, seek and search so as to attain or achieve Realization of Enlightenment *is not,* and *can never be,* a Way of Enlightenment Awakening, but, rather, is utter folly and foolishness. It is a *certain* way to avoid Mind of Nondual Self-as-Self Consciousness Awakening. Do not delude yourself, you cannot *attain* or *achieve* such transcendent Realization, and It cannot be *possessed,* as if It were a dualistic subject-versus-object possession. In *each* and *every* moment there is Awakened Enlightenment Realization. There is *nothing* to seek, search for, or to find; there is *nothing* to attain, achieved, or to possess. You already and always are *That* which you seek and search for. This is, You, and indeed all Consciousness Beings and Entities, are always, already *fully* Enlightened, but seldom if ever Realize This because of self delusion and ignorance, as Buddha Realized and Expressed through His own Enlightenment 2,500 years ago.

Realizing Who and What You Are

I speak to You *directly* now in My own Voice, from *transpersonal* perspective, as Onlinessananda. Ignorant and deluded as I am within my *personal* compound pre-egoic, egoic, and conditioned social-cultural self, I do not speak to You now from *this* self-contracted personal-egoic self or mind of consciousness: Beloved, Recognize that You are *All.* You are That which Is *and* Is-not, *and* is Neither. Recognize this Awakened *Nondual Self* as the True Nature and Condition that You always already are. And, indeed, come to Realize that each and every Consciousness Being and Entity is *always, already* and *completely* this same Enlightened Nature and Condition, is fully this same *Bliss-Divine Revelation Self*

Reality that You are. Come to this Realization of Who and What You are; come to this uncreated, unborn and undying Nondual Self-as-Self Reality Consciousness of All and None You are. This is Your *True Nature, Identity* and *Condition*.

You *are* this *Omnipresent* Consciousness, this Self of *each* and *every* Being and Entity. You are the transcendent *Universal Heart, Psyche,* and *World Soul* of each and all Beings and Entities. All of the joy and sorrow, pain and suffering, wisdom and knowledge, ignorance and delusion that each Being and Entity experiences and knows is *Yours* also, and is *fully* Intuitively Known to You, and thus *fully* Experienced by You as well. There is no *otherness,* no *separateness,* no *we* versus *they* or *I* versus *you* duality of or about You. *Boundless* and *timeless,* You are All and Every, Only and Completely. *This* is Who and What You are, that *You* must come to Recognize and Realize. *This* is the *Awakening from* the dream you now live *as* and *through.* Beloved, Awaken! And dream no more.

When *all* consciousness of predominant-exclusive pre-egoic self, egoic self, and conditioned social-cultural self realities of mind consciousness are surrendered and have died, are transcended but *then* included, You *Realize* the Radiant Emptiness You always have been, now are, and will ever be. This Divinity is the *Suchness* that You *truly* are. Strip away your combined predominant-exclusive pre-egoic, egoic, and conditioned social-cultural compound mask persona. *Transcend,* but also include and integrate within the heights of such transcendence, your compound pre-egoic, egoic, and conditioned social-cultural self realities and consciousness, through this *transpersonal* transcendent Consciousness *Awakening* and *Transformation.* In this Way, negate, and then preserve, the functional importance, strength and power of your pre-personal-egoic, personal-egoic, and conditioned social-cultural compound mind-based self realities, so that now these *serve* and *support* this Realization of Who, *in Truth,* You are.

There is No Fixed and Specific Formula for Enlightenment Awakening

The manifest Form Reality of Your human life embodiment is the

Way of Your Awakening. Thus *Realize*, for Yourself, the day to day Expression of this *unique* and *original* Way of transcendent Transformation that You are. Indeed, You are the *only* One who can come to See and Know this Way of Awakening, that is Yours *alone*. In this Way, the transparent *Means Whereby* is always already completely there before You, just as You *are* right here and now. Such Awakened *Realization* of Nondual Self-as-Self Reality, which Consciousness Reality is *Who,* in Truth, You are, *cannot* be searched for, sought, found, attained, achieved, gained, grasped or possessed. This *Self* of Supreme Reality "thing" has *no thing-ness*; this "other" has *no other-ness* to attain or grasp. You *are* Supreme Reality *Itself,* All and Only, which *cannot* be lost or found.

There is no *fixed formula* for the Way of Enlightenment Awakening, and no *quick* and *easy* answers to be found. No one to certainly and securely tell You how and what to do. Ultimately, this is *Your* Way and *Your* Responsibility. However, as a social human being, you need to look for, and can *greatly* benefit from, the trustworthy, knowledgeable, experienced and wise counsel and advice of others, in *all* domains of human knowledge, expression, awareness and meaning. With such counsel in mind, I would venture the advice to You that an ongoing *meditation practice* is critically important in Nondual Consciousness Awakening. However, please understand that I am *not,* and *cannot* be, Your salvation guru or savior; for *only* You can function so. But I *can* advise and be a spiritual guide and teacher to You, *if* you *earnestly* and *diligently* so chose to consider and apply the Teachings that I offer. But ultimately, it is *only* You who, moment to moment, holds the *Intuitive Key* to Recognition of Your own *original* and *unique* Way of Nondual Spirit-as-Spirit Consciousness Awakening and Realization.

The *relative* and *predominant-exclusive* consciousness of self-contracted compound pre-personal pre-egoic-self, personal-egoic self, and conditioned social-cultural self realities, *cannot* fundamentally guide and inform You in this *transpersonal* Journey of Awakening. Rather, these limited and partial compound personal-egoic self realities of mind and consciousness will easily, and most often, mislead, misdirect and misinform You in this critical regard. Remember, the always, already transcendent

Enlightenment Awakening that you may wish to seek was *never* lost, and so cannot be found. This *Gateless Gate* is always already there, accessibly and immediately before You in *plain* sight; It is always *completely* available and open to You. The *transcendent Way* of Nondual Self-as-Self Realization is trans-pre-egoic (trans-pre-mental and trans-pre-rational), trans-egoic (trans-mental and trans-rational), and also trans-conditioned-social-cultural, in that It *transcends* but then *includes* these three predominant-exclusive and interrelated compound personal-egoic self realities of mind and consciousness.

The Way of Enlightenment is One of Transcendent Compassion and Wisdom

Do you think it will be easy to Realize this *Way* of Enlightenment Awakening, Your Way? *It will not.* Quite the contrary. If you're at all like me, I suspect it will be a *long, hard* and *painful* struggle. Filled with anger, sorrow, regret, delusion, hubris, ignorance and stupidity. Certainly, as pre-egoic, egoic, and conditioned social-cultural compound self realities, it will *not* be simple, quick or easy - or even possible, for that matter, *as* this predominant-exclusive compound personal-egoic self of mind. The *Way* of Enlightenment Awakening, and thus of Onliness as one such Way, is one of transcendent *Compassion* and *Wisdom,* the practice of which, at once, *is* and *is not* (and is neither) simple, quick or easy.

This phrase "is and is not (and is neither)" occurs quite often in this text, and *does not* mean that the designated referent "is and is not (and is neither)" from different perspectives or at different times. It *does not* mean that the referent "is and is not (and is neither)" in different conditions, contexts or circumstances. Rather, it means that the designated referent, at once, "is and is not (and is neither)" from *all* perspectives, at *all* times, and under *all* conditions, contexts and circumstances. Note here, and elsewhere, that in the use of dualistic-contrastive *personal-egoic* language (this language) to describe nondualistic-noncontrastive *transpersonal, trans-egoic* Nondual Self Reality, there will inherently exists a *meaning paradox,* an apparent *self-contradiction,* in the use of such personal-egoic language expression and meaning. This is a function of the either-or, dualistic-contrastive *limitations* of personal-egoic language meaning and expression.

Conditional and Self-Contracted Pre-egoic, Egoic, and Social-Cultural Self Realities

Awakening to Mind of Nondual Consciousness Self Realization will *require* You to transcend, but include *within* such transcendence, conditional and self-contracted pre-personal pre-egoic self, personal egoic self, as well as conditioned social-cultural self and consciousness. That is, You must *die* to, and *Know* the death of, all *three* of these relative and conditioned *surface-structure* compound self realities of mind and consciousness. Make *no* mistake, there is no painless, simple, quick, or easy way around this, nor is there an exception to it. Remember, it is *You* who can and must discover, unveil, embrace and fully occupy Your own Path of *transpersonal* Awakening and, in so doing, *witness* the death of these three predominant-exclusive, relative and narcissistic interrelated compound self realities. Remember, it is *only* You who can Awaken to, and thus fully Realize, this Way of Enlightenment which is *original* and *unique* to You. That is, this *Consciousness Path* of uncontracted, unconditioned and unconditional (i.e., beyond all *relative* conditions and circumstances) Nondual Self-as-Self Reality, which is Your *True* Nature and Condition.

Completely abandoning all personal fears, desires and self importance, *Surrender* to and *Be*, and thus Become, this Radiant transcendent Self of no-self, *beyond* the ignorance and delusion of pre-egoic, egoic and conditioned social-cultural compound personal-egoic self realities. Fully *Acknowledge* and *Embrace* this transpersonal Self You already truly are, have always been and will ever be. In Compassion and Wisdom, *See* this Self Reality of All and Every that You are. *Recognize* that, in Fact, You are *causeless*, *timeless* and *uncreated* Nondual Self of All-pervading Consciousness. This All-encompassing and Boundless Self of *Mystery*. Beloved, open Your Universal Heart and World Soul to these *Revelations* of Truth I tell You now.

Directly Experientially Test for Yourself the Truthfulness of What I Say

But, of course, my simply asserting this as Truth does not make it so. After You have acquired the knowledge, skills and tools to do so, You need to *directly experientially* test these assertions for Yourself, in Your own Way, to *See* if such Revelations are True or False. And then go on to *compare* Your experiential Outcomes and Findings concerning these assertions to the Findings of Your peers, who have also acquired the knowledge, skills and tools required, and then *gone on* to *experientially directly* test the Truth or Falseness of these asserted Revelation, for Themselves. The philosopher Ken Wilber eloquently speaks of *directly experientially*, and in this broad sense empirically, *testing* such transcendental assertions in this way.

Beloved, You are not *just* this relative and conditional socially-culturally conditioned, pre-egoic and egoic *bodymind* self and consciousness. Awaken from this slumbering dream, and sometimes nightmare. And understand that such transcendent Awakening is the *ordeal* and *daunting challenge* I put before You. This is a *radical* Way of spiritual Enlightenment *Awakening, Transformation* and *Transfiguration* that I now ask You to take up and to endure. Very rarely, indeed, is this Path or Way painless or quick or soft or smooth or easy. Almost always, the Awakening ordeal of transpersonal Self *Recognition* and *Realization* is a painful, prolonged, difficult, challenging and often discouraging experience and struggle. And again, It is neither a goal or destination, nor is it a consequence, nor is it something that can be sought after, pursued, found, attained, achieved, granted, gained or possessed.

Enlightenment Awakened Self is Ordinary and Everyday Self

Nondual Consciousness Awakening to Self-as-Self is not grand, exclusive, or distinctly set apart in *any* way, but rather is common, ordinary, and everyday Self. This Awakened Self-as-Self Reality is not something distant, remote and inaccessible, but rather is *present, immediate, close at hand,* and *completely* accessible. Such

Awakening is not elaborate, complex, opaque and obscure, but is plain, transparent and obvious. Such *Remembrance* of this Nondual Self You Truly are, is *not* vague and darkly-shaded in shadow, but luminously *Bright* and *Real*. This is Radiant *everyday Self* of Truth and Bliss.

The Veils of Pre-personal, Personal, and Interpersonal Self that Must Be Lifted

What is it that makes You so certain of the *final truth* of this *mental* worldspace consciousness of mind reality you have been pre-personally, personally, and socially-culturally-interpersonally *conditioned* to believe in? Why are You so *convinced* that this co-created-interpreted conditional and border-bounded bodymind worldspace consciousness you *mentally* live *within* is, indeed, the ultimate and only true reality? What is *beyond* this conditioned and conditional mental point of view, *from* which you see this *one* relative reality *perspective* that you so firmly hold, and are so certain of? And *who* is this that is so certain? In Truth, Who are You? These are *some* of the personal and transpersonal developmental-evolutionary *existential* issues and questions that You will encounter, and will somehow need to address, in Your Consciousness *Awakening to* and *Remembrance of* Nondual Self-as-Self Recognition and Realization.

These are a small number of the questions, issues and concerns that You will confront, and must transpersonally *Respond to* through transcendence but inclusion (negation and preservation), within the struggle and ordeal of Your own Trans-pre-egoic, Trans-egoic, and Trans-conditioned social-cultural Awakening to Nondual Spirit-as-Spirit Consciousness Realization. These are just a few of the emergent developmental-evolutionary realm-wave issues of transcendent Consciousness that will *successively* unfold for You, and that must be *Resolved* within and through this *profound* and *radically* Transformational Awakening, if all goes developmentally well.

The power and blinding force of your own interrelated predominant-exclusive *pre-personal pre-egoic* self of mind (emotional-sexual, impulsive, archaic-magical, pre-rational and hedonic physical-bodily self), as well as your *personal-egoic* self of mind (mental-rational, narcissistic, self-contracted, egocentric bodymind self), and ultimately even your ethnocentric conditioned and conditional co-constructed-interpreted communal-social-cultural *interpersonal* self of mind, will *all* naturally resist their *predominant subordination, supremacy-exclusion* and *death;* which death will occur with the transcendent emergence of *transpersonal* Nondual Self-as-Self Recognition, Remembrance and Realization. What You encounter in this difficult *Transformation* is, at once, a joyous Bliss-Divine Awakening *and* a prolonged and painful compound personal-egoic self *pre-personal, personal,* and *interpersonal* transcendence but inclusion *ordeal,* which is profoundly disruptive, disorienting and daunting - *in the extreme.*

But Awakened *Realization* of Nondual Self-as-Self Reality is *not* something other-than or beyond Your here and now capacity. Indeed, It is the birthless and deathless Self You always already are, and have ever been. It is the *Spirit-as-Spirit* Bliss-Divine Self that You *fully* are, right here and now, but, blinded by self-contracted ignorance, desire, fear and delusion, you do not Recognize this Self. You *are* Christ-consciousness and Buddha-mind, and Know It not. As compound personal-egoic self, you live in the blindness and confusion of egocentric, narcissistic illusion and fantasy, and See it not. Numb and slumbering, you sleepwalk in a shadow dream, that is a *nightmare* of your own making and design, and yet you *think* you are awake!

Pre-personal, Personal, and Interpersonal Social-Cultural Maturity and Integration

However, can you also see the necessity for a developmentally mature, skilled, strong and perceptive *pre-personal* physical-bodily self, *personal* bodymind-egoic self, and *interpersonal* communal social-cultural self, in order to *endure* the ordeal of, and Surrender to, this *radical* Transformation of *transpersonal* Nondual Self-as-Self Awakening? This is *why* the spiritual practice that You define, develop and sustain, so as to facilitate such Awakening to

Self Reality, must also include, as an *integral* dimension of this practice, practices that support and encourage the growth and development toward maturity, insight, strength and perceptiveness of your *pre-personal, personal* and *interpersonal* compound self realities of mind and consciousness. And this is so, even though *predominant-exclusive* identification *with* and *as* each of these separate-self-sense relative, conditioned and conditional compound self realities *must* finally and completely die, must be negated and preserved, *within* Nondual Self-as-Self Consciousness Recognition, Remembrance and Realization.

But Understand, that these three predominant-exclusive and single-perspective functioning compound personal-egoic self realities of conditioned and conditional *pre-personal, personal* and *interpersonal-social-cultural* mind reality, are *also* Self Itself, and none of Than. In Truth, they have no *other-ness* or *separateness* from transcendent Self Reality about them. For human beings, these limited and relative compound personal-egoic self realities are the consciousness wellsprings *through, but not by,* which transcendental Consciousness Awakening emerges and finds Expression. Thus, because of their self-contracted limitations and conditionality, they *all* must be transcended, but then included *within* such transpersonal Consciousness transcendence.

The Ascent of Transcendent Wisdom and Descent of Immanent Compassion

How do You *Recognize* Your Way of Enlightenment Awakening in the conditioned and conditional complexity and confusion of your earth-centered human life? *Follow* the transpersonal Awareness and Experience of Your own *Intuitive* Heart and Mind. Meditate in solitude and stillness, *through* Emptiness. And so, Awaken to this *incandescent* Self of Emptiness, which Embraces *both* the transcendent Wisdom and immanent Compassion You always already are. Do not let yourself be turned away from this Truth-Consciousness Bliss-Divine *Self Identity* of Wisdom and Compassion, that, in Reality, You *are*.

Let conditional self *Surrender* to, and thus *Embrace,* these two *Luminous Beacons* and *Directions* of Spirit, of Self. That is, turn toward and open Your Heart-Soul to the transcendent *Ascent* of Wisdom and Truth, and to the immanent *Descent* of Compassion, Care and Loving Kindness toward *all* Consciousness Beings and Entities. *This* is where You can *start* and, indeed, where You can *end* as well. In Truth, these two *directional* Realities are *one* and the *same.* They are the two Radiant Sides of one and the same Coin of Awakened Enlightenment Consciousness.

The Immanent Descent of Compassion, Concern, and Care for each and all Consciousness Beings and Entities is at the very *core* of, is *central* to, the Way of Awakening to Nondual Self-as-Self Consciousness Reality. But, of course, this is speaking of transcendent Self from a polarized subject-versus-object *singular perspective* point of view, through and within the pre-transcendental conditional consciousness of *relative* compound personal-egoic self reality. Remember, that Self of unconditional *Absolute Reality* has *no* separateness or other-ness *of, about*, or *to* It. Spirit-as-Spirit Awakened Nondual Realization *is* the World and, indeed, is *beyond* all Worlds, without a second or exception or exclusion. Beloved, You *are* the World, and all Worlds, and there is nothing *separate* from You or *other-than* You. There is no *we* and *they,* no *I* and *you,* no *mine* and *yours*. In Truth, You always, already are *each, every* and *all* Consciousness Beings and Entities, totally and completely.

Bliss-Divine Consciousness of Nondual Self-as-Self, this All-knowledge and All-beings Omnipresent Self Reality that You *Innately* are, *Intuitively* Comprehends the essential transpersonal Meaning and Import of all Beings' and Entities' singular perspectives, and all at once. And You, as Perceiver-and-that-which-is-Perceived, are the *singular* Truth of this Nondual Self Comprehensive Insight. You *are* this All-pervasive and All-knowing transcendental Omni-presence, if only You will *open* Your Eyes and Awaken to It. And yet, you blindly linger on in isolated, self-contracted and egocentric darkness and delusion. Blinded to Your own Christ-consciousness and Enlightened Buddha-mind, you *slumber* in vacant, shallow, fragmented-shattered dreams. But, as Self of Brahman-Atman, You are and Embrace (transcend but include) *even* these fragmented and self-contracted dreams.

The Vision and Means-whereby of One's Unique Awakening

What I present and describe to You here, is the necessary and sufficient broad *potential* Vision of the Ground and Opening *from* and *within* which You can *Remember* and *Realize* Your own original transcendental Pathway of Nondual Consciousness Mind Awakening. As Teacher and Guide, what I here Confess and Reveal to You is a *Vision* of Your Bliss-Divine *True* Nature and Condition, and, with This, point out an abstract-outline *Means-whereby*, a Way, through which You may come to Nondual Self Truth-consciousness Awakening. But it is *You* who must *transpersonally* come to actually *See* and *Define* this broad Vision, and then come to *Act Upon* and *Realize* this Means-whereby, *on* Your own and *for* Yourself. Your Awakening is *uniquely* Yours alone.

Beloved, again, if your suffering and despair primarily involves problems of psychosocial-emotional confusion and disorder, which occur within the realm-waves of pre-personal-pre-egoic, personal-egoic, and conditioned social-cultural compound self of mind consciousness, carefully consider seeking psychological counseling and psychotherapy. Find a trusted, knowledgeable and insightful pre-egoic, egoic, and conditioned socially-culturally *aware* counselor or psychotherapist who identifies with and understands your current life situation and perspective. And then work with that person to confront, explore and resolve, so as to *consciously* recognize, acknowledge and re-integrate into your pre-personal, personal-egoic and interpersonal conditioned social-cultural compound self, these *subconscious* shadow dimensions of alienation, suppression, projection, denial and repression.

Remember, in Onliness theory and perspective, the development-evolution of a conscious, mature, strong and integrated compound *pre-personal-pre-egoic* self, *personal-egoic* bodymind self, and *interpersonal* conditioned social-cultural self are *certainly*, but indirectly, important in support and facilitation of *transpersonal trans-egoic* Self Awakening and Realization. Also, understand that continuing development and growth of your compound *personal-egoic* self's mind of intellectual-mental learning, insight and understanding, in *all areas* of knowledge and wisdom, is of significant importance in the developmental facilitation of *transpersonal* Nondual Self-as-Self Revelation. And note as well, that careful and sustained practice of *personal* physical body-life health, development and wellbeing (e.g., nutrition, exercise, rest and sleep) are also of significant importance in support and facilitation of such *transpersonal* Recognition and Realization.

However, avoid becoming *obsessively* concerned and preoccupied with the mere *vehicle* of *personal* physical-body and bodymind and *interpersonal* social-cultural surface functioning and expression, which are of relative and conditional compound personal-egoic self reality. Clearly Understand, that these relative and self-contracted personal and conditioned social-cultural realities of body, mind, and social-cultural community, if excessively pursued, obsessed about, and predominantly identified with, will *certainly* remove You from Your Path of *transpersonal* Nondual Self-as-Self Awakening and Realization. These are not the Way of Enlightenment. Remember that, as Sri Nisargadatta Maharaj reminds us, You are *not* your body, You are *not* your mind.

Observe and Monitor the Functioning of Narcissus

Without becoming overwhelmed, simply do as much as, and the best that, you can, in this moment here and now. Carefully witness and observe narcissus. See *how* your own self-centered, self-justifying compound personal-egoic self of mind *meanders* in each moment throughout the day. *Monitor* your own *ego-defensive* ideation, maneuvering and reactivity. *Observe* your egocentric based self-proclamations and self-assertions, as well as your subtle gestures and posturing of *self-importance* in your relationships with other people. *Observe* and *monitor* your slavish imitative copying, echoing and mimicking of what others say and do; *witness* your personal-egoic petty envies, jealousies, flares of anger, projections, impatience, likes-dislikes, distastes, superficial judgments and distains. Observe your self-centered cruelty, blindness and indifference toward the condition and circumstance of other consciousness Beings and Entities. *See* your *dualistic* compound personal-egoic self's functioning moment to moment as *central subject,* with *all* else around it, including fellow Beings, as *mere objects.* These are just a few of the critical *narcissistic themes* to be observed and monitored in One's compound personal-egoic self's existential life.

Finding a Wise and Compassionate Teacher and Guide

Whatever *integral* spiritual life practice you may choose to undertake in Awakening to Nondual Spirit-as-Spirit Consciousness, I would encourage You to *seek out* and *be open to* at least one compassionate, knowledgeable, truthful and experienced teacher and guide. And then to carefully listen to, learn from, and be guided by such a teacher and guide. This is *so* important in my view. It is also important, if at all possible, to seek out, find and share your life practice with others, your peers, who share a similar perspective and practice to your own. Such integral life practice *sharing with* and *support from* others, who identify with your own practice, values and worldspace Consciousness, can be *so* helpful; it can, especially at times of compound personal-egoic self-doubt and discouragement, be *invaluable.*

The Nature and Concerns of One's Spiritual Integral Life Practice

In time, You can and will discover, unfold and realize an emerging and evolving spiritual integral life practice that *facilitates* Awakening from the delusional pre-egoic, egoic and conditioned social-cultural self slumber, which most earth-centered humans call reality. In any case, the spiritual life practice that You chose to follow will *require* great self discipline and persistence. It is often an *ordeal* that is intense, prolonged, uneven, confusing, painful and difficult. But, as I've said, this ordeal is also *within* Your capacity to recognize, follow, endure, appreciate, and even celebrate, in each and every moment. Ultimately, however, Your specific spiritual integral life practice *Pathway* is definable and describable *only* by

You, and You alone. It is finally and uniquely *Your* transcendental Path and Destiny, or Karma.

Moment to moment, *study* and *observe* what this integral life practice *is,* in its unfolding. What is it telling You about Your daily life? What *discovered* knowledge, insights and implications does its evolving emergent content have *in* and *for* You, day to day? How does this content *relate* and *apply* to Your Awakening from predominant-exclusive pre-egoic, personal-egoic, and conditioned social-cultural compound self ignorance and delusion? And how can the *directives* of this discovered knowledge and insight be *practically* assimilated and integrated into Your *overall* integral life practice, so as to *further* facilitate Your Awakening to Nondual Self-as-Self Consciousness Reality?

Do not be fearful of *Intuitively following* to where it is Your spiritual life practice directs and points, and, in this way, *leads* You. Be mindful that it is primarily your own *self-inflicted* doubt, criticism and distrust, concerning Your integral life practice Awakening Pathway, that *You* will have to confront and *must* transcend, but also account for and include *within* such transcendence. This doubt and distrust *derives* primarily from the self-contracted and fearful consciousness of compound personal-egoic self ignorance and delusion. *Recognize* that You *are* the Kosmos Itself (and Beyond) in Its All-ness and Onliness, and have ever Been and will always Be. You are the *Many* and the *One*, and also this *Mystery* of *Emptiness* and *None*. In Mind Truth-consciousness Reality, there is *nothing* at all for You to fear. And in relation to priorities, what exactly is it that's *more* fundamental and important than Enlightenment Consciousness Awakening and Realization?

One's Complete Commitment to Self Revelation and Transformation

What *is* it that ultimately holds you back from *fully* revealing, engaging and embracing Your spiritual integral life practice of *Awakening* to Nondual Self-as-Self Reality and Truth? What is it that keeps you from *complete* commitment to, and involvement in, Your integral life practice of Bliss-Divine Self *Remembrance* and

Recognition? In my view, these are *basic* questions that You need to ask Yourself, and then, in discovery, reveal *to* Yourself, the answers *for* Yourself.

Can you realistically expect to confront and endure the ordeal of *transcending* but including (within the context of such transcendence) compound pre-personal-pre-egoic, personal-egoic, and conditioned social-cultural consciousness self realities, *without* the Revelations which derive from application of the *self-discipline, earnestness, fearlessness, desirelessness, vigilance, commitment, self-sacrifice,* and *persistence,* which are *so* basic to Your World Soul, and Spirit based integral life practice? My Teachings *certainly* encourage such application of self-discipline, earnestness, desirelessness, sustained commitment, persistence, vigilance, self-sacrifice, and fearlessness within Your spiritual life practice of *Transformational* Self Awakening. Each day then, moment-to-moment, apply these powerful "tools" as best you can, to *release* Yourself from narcissistic compound personal-egoic mind of self and consciousness; so as to *abandon* Your relative and conditional egocentric-based emotional reactions and mental ideation, in both interior thought and exterior expression. Each day, attempt to consciously include and integrate these bold Means-whereby *applications* into Your daily life and practice.

In Meditation, You Recognize and Remember the Bliss-Divine Self You already are

You are, right here and now, *selfless Self* of Bliss-Divine Awareness and Experience. You are this *Realization Self* of Wisdom and Compassion, always and already. Most often, this will *initially* become Apparent to You in meditation, as You Awaken to Pure Emptiness. I would encourage You, in meditation, to ongoingly and repeatedly inquire of Yourself with the question, "Who am I? In sustained meditation, more and more, You Recognize and Remember this Divinity of Bliss You are, which is Your *deep* and *innate* True Nature and Condition. This is one reason why the Peace, Solitude and Freedom of such quiet and mindful daily meditation is *so* important in my view.

But understand, in Onliness theory and perspective, meditation is not itself a *means* to some *end* or *goal,* like transcendental Awakening, Enlightenment, and so on. Meditation is an *End* in and of itself. In Onliness, mindful and quiet meditation *is* Enlightenment *Itself,* is *Itself* Awakening to Nondual Self-as-Self Consciousness Realization. Such meditation is *not* some sort of relative and conditional *seeking* and *searching* method, technique or means, so as to attain, gain, achieve or find a "state" identified as Enlightenment. To begin with, Mind Enlightenment *is not* a state among other states of Consciousness, but rather is the *Wellspring, Ground* and *Condition* of *all* states of Consciousness. So, in meditation, You are not *seeking* or *finding* anything at all. Authentic meditation occurs *in* and *of* and *for* Itself; it is an *End* unto Itself alone.

Awaken to God-consciousness Self of Wisdom and Compassion that You Truly are

This *selfless* Self of Bliss-Divinity You are *does not* depend upon conditions, causes, seeking, doing, attainment, nor on this or that *state* of consciousness. You are the *Consciousness of God* right here and now. As the sage Sri Ramana Maharshi has said: "The Self itself is God." You always already are *God-consciousness Self* of Supreme Wisdom and Compassion, but You must, in Fact, Awaken to and Realize this *Supreme Self Identity.* From a *personal-temporal* bodymind point of view, such Bliss-Divine Self Identity *Realization* can occur in a nanosecond, or could require a million lifetimes. In Truth, such transcendent Mind of Awakened Self Realization is *beyond* and *prior to* time and space, is not at all a *process* or *function* of space-time. And such *Awakening* is neither easy, nor is It difficult, and *both*; such *Realization* is neither unattainable, nor is It attainable, and both.

Observe yourself, observe how you function in everyday worldspace mind of relative consciousness existence. *Witness,* and *See* for yourself, the here and now temporal comings and goings of your immediate compound pre-egoic, egoic, and socially-culturally conditioned *relative* life and self realities of mind consciousness. Become intimately and acutely aware of, and *directly experience,* your anger, hate, greed, delusion, ignorance, fear, envy, jealousy, self-importance, self-aggrandizement, self-superiority, impatience, resentment, vindictiveness, manipulativeness, stupidity, hypocrisy, indifference, cruelty, selfishness, self-centeredness, and self-righteousness, which so often emerge and manifest in self of conditional and relative consciousness existence. *Recognize* and *acknowledge* the specific nature and functioning of your moment-to-moment conditioned and conditional compound self's self-contracted expressions and responses. Such mind monitoring and observation is the initial *Means-whereby* basis of *relative* compound self and consciousness *transcendence* but inclusion; this is the initial Transformational Way of compound pre-egoic self, egoic self, and conditioned social-cultural self *negation* and preservation (within such *transpersonal* negation).

Luminous Divine-Self of All and Each is One's Ineffable Non-abiding True Identity

What I speak of here to You is beyond *pre-mental, mental-rational,* and *conditioned social-cultural* self assimilation-identity; it is *trans-mental, trans-rational, trans-conceptual,* and *trans-social-cultural.* Awakening to Nondual Self-as-Self Consciousness Realization *transcends,* but includes within such Realization (and in this Way negates and preserves), *all* pre-mental-conceptual, mental-conceptual, and conditioned social-cultural mental-conceptual expression and assimilation-identity, but only *as* and *within* this transcendent Self Awakening. This Uncreated and Timeless *Bliss-Divine Awakened Self* of Absolute Radiant Emptiness, that *You* are in this very moment, is trans-mental, trans-rational and trans-conceptual in Nature. This *Self,* which, *at once,* is both Form and Formless, and is neither, is *Who* and *What* You are in Truth. It is Your Non-abiding *True Identity.* In this way, Nondual Consciousness Self-as-Self is the *fathomless* Open Ground and Source *of,* and as such is *prior to,* all temporal and relative pre-personal-pre-egoic-conceptual, personal-egoic-conceptual, and conditioned social-cultural-conceptual manifestations, realizations and self-identities.

Beloved, You are *All, Every* and *Each,* and thus bounded, limited and contained by *None*. You are both Alpha and Omega, and at once Neither. You are the *Liberation* and *Freedom* of Brahman-Atman Consciousness alone; and, as Such, You are unknowable, ineffable, unfathomable, and infinitely beyond compound pre-personal-pre-egoic, personal-egoic, and conditioned social-cultural consciousness self *understanding* and *identity*. You are, right now, this *Luminous Divine Self* of Intuition, Light and Revelation. The incandescent *Beacon* of Worlds.

Your Integral Spiritual Life Practice *is* Your Everyday Life

Can You doubt that, in Reality, You *are* this unqualifable *Suchness*? Do not. This is Your, and each and every Consciousness Being's and Entity's, *inherent* Nature, Condition, and Identity. This *Bliss-Divine Self* You are, *is* Mind of Nondual Supreme Reality and Truth. And, within Your transcendental spiritual integral life practice, You are invited to Discover this *for* Yourself, in *this* life here and now.

But understand, Your integral life practice *is* Your own moment-to-moment *everyday life* itself, and not an object-entity "practice" that is *other* to You, and that You somehow occupy, assume or take up. This *evolving* integral life practice that *You* discover and unfold, which is the *transformational* basis of Your transpersonal Freedom and Liberation, is not some "thing" that You *do*, but, rather, is a *Way* of life and living. It is not some *technique* that You use to attain some object-entity "goal," but rather is *Itself* Awakening Self Revelation.

Most importantly, within your relative earth-centered human consciousness existence, start with the self-sacrifice of serving other Consciousness Beings and Entities, however *not* as a means, but rather as an End unto itself. Start by being of *selfless* Compassionate service and help to other Consciousness Entities and Beings. Actively involve Yourself in this Way, within this *Sacred* existential World. Make this *central* in and to Your integral life practice. This, of course, is the immanent Descent of Compassion *Expression* of Enlightenment Awakening, within manifest Form Reality. This is

Your *response* of Loving Kindness, Care and Compassion to each and every Consciousness Entity and Being, including Yourself. This selfless and unconditional response and action is *inherently* a critical integral Dimension of the Way of Enlightenment Awakening and Realization within Onliness theory and perspective.

The Gateless Gate of Self Remembrance and Revelation Is Always Already Open

In Awakening to *Radiant Self* of Bliss Illumination, there is no *doing* to be done. There's *nothing* to be sought for, accomplished or achieved. There is no *place* to go *or* to come from, and also no place to abide. Indeed, there is *no separate self* to do such abiding, coming or going. There *is* no place where this timeless and boundless Self You are is not *already there,* as both *All* of place and *None* of place. As Awakened All-embracing Self, separate *subject versus object* polarity-duality is transcended but included, and so does not arise or occur in Consciousness. Nondual Self-as-Self Remembrance has no otherness, no separateness, no second or opposite, no some-thing-ness, and no no-thing-ness. And, at the same time, such an Awakened Self is certainly *all* of these designations also. And so, You have *no* problem or dilemma to confront, engage or solve. Do You See how transparent, simple, and easy the gateless gate of Realized Enlightenment Awakening really is? It is a gateless gate always and already *open,* as the inherent *Ground* and *Wellspring* of Your very Nature and Condition.

Nondual Self Awakening Completely Ends All Personal Self-Imposed Suffering

When compound *pre-personal* (pre-egoic), *personal* (egoic), and socially-culturally-conditioned *interpersonal* realm-wave self realities of mind consciousness are *transcended,* but included *within* One's transpersonal Consciousness Self Realization, there occurs an end to *all* personal suffering. But, of course, as an *embodied* Being of manifest Form Reality, even within realm-wave levels of *transpersonal* Consciousness Awakening, there will remain and occur bodymind-personal injury, pain, aging, disease and death. These are all inherent to human *manifest* temporal embodiment.

However, *suffering* is the personal bodymind's *self-imposed* mental-emotional *reactions* of self-contraction, fear, anger, resentment, dread, anxiety and sorrow *to* the bodymind's injury, pain, aging, disease and death. These relative, conditioned and conditional mental-emotional *self-imposed* reactions simply *no longer* arise or occur in Consciousness with One's Awakening to birthless and deathless transcendent Nondual Spirit-as-Spirit Consciousness Realization.

Experientially Engage Your Whole Self in Your Integral Life Practice of Awakening

My essential message to You is to *discover, embrace* and *unfold* within Your spiritual integral life practice, Your own *unique* Way or Path of Awakening to Nondual Self of Consciousness Realization. That is, to directly *experientially* engage Your whole Self - body, emotional, mental, World Soul and Spirit - in the sequence of progressively Consciousness-inclusive developmental-evolutionary realm-wave *states* and *stages* of Spirit or Self. In Onliness theory, such development-evolution is from *personal* advanced vision-logic realm-wave consciousness to *transpersonal* Psychic Multi-istence, to Subtle Prim-istence, to Causal Holistence realm-waves of transcendent Consciousness. And then, development-evolution *beyond* (and including) all of these realm-waves, to and as Nondual Self-as-Self Consciousness Awakening and Realization (see Figures 2, 3, 4, 5. 6 and 7).

You are Fully and Completely this Truth-Consciousness Awakening, Here and Now

The *Liberated Mind* Enlightenment of Nondual Self-as-Self Consciousness includes Realization of the *delusion* of separate subject-object polarity-duality. As *Awakened Self* of Truth-consciousness, separate *subject* versus *object* polarity-duality perception no longer arises of occurs in Consciousness. This is so because, beyond the illusion of polarity-duality's subject-object separateness, You are always and already *All* and *Each* and *Every,* at once and only. As indicated, there exists no otherness or separateness within or *of* Nondual Consciousness Awakening. And it is *You* who are *fully* and *completely* this very Consciousness Reality of Self, right here and now. In This, please understand that You are neither a *portion*, *part*, or *representation* of this Nondual Self Reality, nor an *expression* or *reflection* of such Truth-Consciousness. Rather, You are the *whole* Totality, the All and Every, of this Bliss-Divine Nondual Spirit-as-Spirit Consciousness of Mind, always and already. You are none other than God-consciousness and Christ-consciousness *Itself*, utterly, completely and only.

But do *not* imagine, or attempt to suppose or pretend, that you are Awakened Nondual Consciousness Self Reality and Truth *as long as* you are, and your *core* identity remains, within predominant-exclusive *bodymind* *identified* and *oriented* pre-personal, personal-egoic or conditioned social-cultural compound self and consciousness. To pretend in this way is disastrous *folly* and unbridled *delusion* on your part. You have *first* the formidable challenge and ordeal to completely *transcend*, but include from this higher transcendent Consciousness, your mind of interactive and interrelated compound pre-personal, personal-egoic, and socially-culturally conditioned *relative* self realities of consciousness.

The Centrality of Compassion, Communion and Wisdom in Your Everyday Practice

Central to Onliness and Its spiritual integral life practice are *Compassion, Communion* and *Wisdom*; which Wisdom is identified as *transcendent* Knowledge and Meaning in Onliness theory and perspective. These designations are presented and symbolized within the *cardinal* Psychic Multi-istence Consciousness rings of combined Figures 3 and 5, and graphically in Figures 6 and 7. These *three* transcendental Dimensions need to unfold and develop *in application,* within and through what the philosopher Ken Wilber calls the four quadrants of existence that are always present in *relative* and *conditional* human holonic Consciousness manifestation.

Thus, at least in the *Way* of Onliness Awakening, it is important that You *center* and *focus* Your integral life practice within the Mind of Compassion, Communion and Wisdom (which includes Truth), so that these three *core* transpersonal Dimensions are *Realized* and find *Expression* in and through the compound personal-egoic self's four relative and conditional *pre-transcendental mind consciousness* quadrants (described by Ken Wilber) of: individual interior subjective "I" awareness and experience, individual exterior objective "IT" awareness and experience, communal interior intersubjective cultural "WE" awareness and experience, and collective exterior interobjective social-structural "ITS" awareness and experience. But understand, that these *mentally* conceived *distinct* and *separate* four quadrants of compound personal-egoic self reality and consciousness do not arise, occur or exist within the *trans-mental* ultimate Reality of Awakened Nondual Self-as-Self Consciousness Enlightenment.

In summary then, it's important that You include work within Your spiritual integral life practice that embraces and engages *all* Consciousness realm-waves of body-life, emotional-sexual, mental-cognitive, World Soul, and Spirit Reality levels. And that this is accomplished *throughout* Your developmental-evolutionary *discovery*, *unfolding* and *application* of these three core transpersonal Dimensions of Compassion, Communion and Wisdom. But, also, all of these above five realm-waves levels of Consciousness, in relation to these three above *transpersonal* Dimensions, need to be *employed* in practice *within* and *throughout* all four of the *personal* holonic quadrants of individual-interior-subjective, individual-exterior-objective, communal-cultural-interior-intersubjective, and social-structural-exterior-interobjective *existential* dimensions of *relative* and *conditional* pre-transcendental compound personal-egoic self and consciousness.

The Importance of an Ongoing and Sustained Meditation Practice

Early on in Your spiritual integral life practice, I would encourage You to look *deeply inward*, through meditation and contemplation, so as to begin to See *beyond* and *through* your narcissistic superficial-surface pre-personal, personal-egoic, and conditioned social-cultural levels of self and mind consciousness. In my view, such ongoing, sustained, quiet and mindful meditation-contemplation is *critical* to the transcendence but inclusion of these three *surface* realm-wave levels of relative compound personal-egoic self and consciousness. Among the several authentic and effective approaches to, and ways of, meditation-contemplation, it's important that You discover *for Yourself* which approach and way, or ways, *most* effectively facilitates Your own *transpersonal* Awakening and Transformation. For myself, I have discovered that the way of serene reflection meditation, as practiced in the Soto Zen Buddhist tradition, has been very helpful.

In this meditation approach, One sits still, quiet and awake, upright, and straight but relaxed, while facing and looking at a blank wall, with legs crossed, and with right and left thumb tips and finger tips touching so as to create a circle, with hands resting on one's lap, and with this circle centered just below the navel. *Just* sit, *just* look; let ideas, thoughts, images, sensations, and emotions *arise* and *pass* - don't *hang on* to these and don't *push* them away. Sit still. If mind wanders in any direction, promptly come back to focusing attention *solely* on the sensations of breathing and breath. Surrender complete focus and attention to *blank* Nothingness, to deep and profound Emptiness. This *pure* Emptiness attention is a *direct* Recognition and Expression of transcendent Awakening.

Releasing Predominant-Exclusive Identification With One's Narcissistic Self Realities

In Realization of Nondual *Self-as-Self* Awakening there occurs a *radical* and *complete* Transformation of Consciousness, wherein the narcissistic *surface levels* of self or mind become at once *transparent* and fully *apparent* as to their relative *emptiness, blindness* and *superficial* nature. In this way, You clearly *Recognize* the Opportunity and Opening to release predominant-exclusive identification *with* and *as* these narcissistic surface compound personal-egoic self realities of consciousness. And through this

Recognition, You come to directly *See* and *Embrace* Your true Nature, Condition, and Identity, which is *of* and *as* Bliss-Radiant Nondual Self Reality *Truth-consciousness.*

But please understand, that the *individual interior subjective* focus of meditation *in* and *of* itself is a function of only *one* of the *four* relative and conditional *pre-transcendental* consciousness quadrants of One's spiritual integral life practice. In this way, as the philosopher Ken Wilber carefully points out, One's interior subjective meditation *interpretations* and *insights* are often blind to, are unconscious of, the *influence* that these other three *conditioned socially-culturally related* quadrants (i.e., conditioned communal-cultural interior intersubjective, conditioned social-societal-structural exterior interobjective, and conditioned individual exterior objective -*conditioned* because this quadrant is embedded in and exposed to extensive exterior-external social-cultural conditioning) has upon such individual interior subjective meditation interpretations and insights. Specifically, One is often personally *blind to*, is unaware of, the content influences that the other *three* relative and conditioned *socially-culturally related* quadrants have upon such individual interior subjective meditation interpretation and insight. Of course, in Awakened Nondual Self of transcendent Truth, there is *no* interior or exterior, *no* inside versus outside; in Supreme Reality there is no *internal* versus *external* polarity-duality.

It is, then, the unrecognizable, and thus unacknowledgedable, *subconscious* and *unconscious* content influences of these three conditioned socially-culturally related quadrants *upon* the quadrant of individual interior subjective meditation interpretation and insight that can, and will, substantially *distort* and *falsify* the Revelations and Truthfulness of such meditation content. Thus, meditation, *by itself*, no matter how long or intensely it is practiced, *cannot* and *will not fully* enable and allow You to Awaken to Nondual Self-as-Self Consciousness Realization.

And this is why You will need to Unveil and Consciously Reveal, and thus *transcend* but include, the distorting influential *subconscious* contents of *all three* conditioned *socially-culturally related* pre-transcendental compound personal-egoic self and consciousness quadrants. That is, these three importantly subconscious, and thus Truth-consciousness distorting, quadrants of conditioned socially-culturally related content *must* be revealed, confronted and transpersonally transcended but included by You, over the developmental-evolutionary course of such Transformational *transcendental* Self-as-Self Remembrance and Realization. The Means-whereby of such Revelation and transcendence but inclusion will shortly be discussed.

In Meditation, Truth Itself Becomes Progressively Apparent and Transparent

Nonetheless, individually-interiorly-subjectively, as You turn more deeply *inward* in meditation there will progressively occur greater *Clarity* of transcendental Insight, Discernment and Understanding. With the *expanding* Consciousness inclusiveness that occurs through meditation, You will more distinctly and readily See and Comprehend the *Sacred* transcendental Nature and Condition of *all* of manifest and unmanifest Reality. And thus, through this more profound Clarity and Comprehension, You are, in Your daily life, enabled to be more Attentive and Responsive in relation to *all* Consciousness Beings and Entities. And in this way, You are able to more effectively See and Act in the *Light* of Truth and Righteousness, *with* and *through* Compassion, Communion and Wisdom. In meditation, as You more and more Realize the infinite and timeless *Radiant Emptiness* You utterly are, Truth Itself becomes more and more *Apparent* and *Transparent* to You. Though *not* the function, goal or purpose of meditation, such meditation yet provides profound *transformational Clarifications* of Your own *relative* and *self-constricted* pre-personal pre-egoic, personal-egoic, and, to some extent, even Your conditioned social-cultural compound self realities and consciousness.

Become Aware of, Sensitive, and Responsive to the Suffering of All Beings

Trust and *follow* this emerging inward *Light* of transcendental Clarity and Discernment. Let Its Universal Radiance outwardly emerge, so as to transpersonally Illuminate Your so called *exterior* personal and social-cultural self *actions, awareness* and *understanding*. As meditation depth of Consciousness inclusiveness increases, You will become more and more Attuned and Sensitive to the suffering of other Consciousness Entities and Beings within your embodied-life earth-centered relative mind reality. That is, You will more and more *directly* Realize and Experience the *severity* and *intensity* of suffering, pain, anguish, rage, fear, remorse, sorrow, regret, dread, terror, helplessness and hopelessness that *other* Consciousness Beings and Entities encounter and live with in this conditional and conditioned world of birth and death.

With the emergence of this Illuminating trans-egoic *Intuitive Awareness* and *Sensitivity* to Others' suffering, You come to *fully* and *selflessly* Comprehend and Understand, and in this way have greater Love and Compassion for, other Consciousness Beings and Entities within your temporal life experience. And, in turn, You come to *Act* and *Serve* with greater *Loving Kindness, Sacrifice* and *Care* toward other Consciousness Beings and Entities, so as to end, or at least lessen, Their pain and suffering. This is Self's or Spirit's Realization, *Your* Realization, of the *Descent* of immanent Compassion *in* and *as* the World. This *is* the Awakening of Enlightenment. And, of course, this Directional Realization of *Compassion, Sacrifice* and *Care* still *further* Illuminates and Clarifies Your *overall* transcendental Insight, Discernment, and Understanding.

In this Way, Your integral spiritual life practice *facilitates* transcendental development-evolution through progressively higher or deeper *sequential* holon-polar realm-waves of Mind Awakening, Devotion and Realization. Put otherwise, this integral life practice *facilitation* thus occurs through progressively more Consciousness inclusive *transpersonal* sequential realm-waves of Wisdom and Compassion (see Figures 3, 4, 5, 6 and 7). And, as suggested, throughout *all* of the Onliness postulated developmental-evolutionary realm-waves of Consciousness Awakening, One's spiritual life practice needs to be *integral* and *comprehensive,* so as to include body life, emotional-sexual life, cognitive-mental life, as well as World Soul and transcendent Spirit

Life Consciousness Realities.

What Exactly is Involved in an Integral and Comprehensive Spiritual Life Practice?

Even though You are *not* your body, it is not Your True Identity, I would suggest and advise that such an *integral* spiritual life practice requires that You carefully, though not obsessively, attend to body-self health and wellbeing, through daily physical activity and exercise involving the whole physical body. Also, that You eat a *balanced* nutritious *vegetarian diet* of healthful and uncontaminated food and drink, get sufficient daily sleep, rest, and relaxation, work in a vocation that embraces Compassion, and that is *life nurturing* and *life positive-supportive* in nature, support and live within an earth-ecologically *balanced* and *sustainable* environment with clean air and pure water, in an earth that is *not* over populated, and carefully avoid intake of substances detrimental to bodily health and wellbeing. I suggest that You follow the Buddha's Middle Way of *moderation* in all matters of bodily health and wellbeing, and, indeed, in *all* dimensions and elements of Your spiritual integral life practice.

Also, even though You are *not* your emotional-sexual self, it is not Your True Self Reality or Identity, I would suggest that an integral and comprehensive spiritual life practice *requires* development of emotional-sexual awareness, perceptiveness, responsiveness, openness, balance and experience, which, in turn, facilitates emotional-sexual wellbeing and maturity. In this way, development of Your *emotional-sexual intelligence* through cultivation of *emotional-sexual* openness, empathy, sensitivity, insight, understanding, expressiveness, intuition, transparency, and especially truthfulness and freedom, is so important. Beloved, understand that *all* of these emotional-sexual dimensions are very important to One's Descent of immanent *Compassion* for each and every Consciousness Being and Entity. The courageous *cultivation* of such *truthful* and *self-revealing personal* emotional-sexual functioning requires sustained practice and application *in relationship*. Such cultivation is the central functional *means-whereby* and *measure of* Your compound personal-egoic self's emotional-sexual equanimity, maturity and wellbeing, which, in turn, is so important *in* and *to* Your *transpersonal* spiritual Awakening.

Again, if you experience troubling and persistent psychosocial-emotional problems and concerns, seek a trusted, knowledgeable and experienced pre-personal, personal-egoic and conditioned social-cultural *insightful* psychological counselor for counseling-psychotherapy. And then, *intently* pursue such personal counseling-psychotherapy until you have recognized, understood and resolved such problems, which primarily manifest at the realm-wave levels of compound pre-personal pre-egoic, personal-egoic, and conditioned social-cultural relative *bodymind* self realities and consciousness.

And even though You are *not* your mind, it is not Your Truth-consciousness Awakened Identity and Self, within pre-transcendental mental-cognitive compound personal-egoic self and consciousness I would encourage You to embrace a compassionate worldcentric *cognitive-mental* point of view. And, certainly, to be an *observant* student, as You study in *all* areas of knowledge, meaning and understanding. Daily immerse Yourself through in-depth study, reading, listening, discussing, observing, and interpreting knowledge and meaning in *every* content area. This would include the physical and social sciences, music, mathematics, all of the arts, literature and poetry, philosophy (from pre-modern to modern to post-modern), cultural studies and the humanities, the biological sciences, and in all of the great mystical and spiritual traditions of the world (including Buddhism, Hinduism, Christianity, Islam, Judaism, Taoism, Baha'i Faith); and also *carefully* study the writing of the world's great transcendental spiritual sages, adepts and philosophers, past and present.

Of course, each human being, by virtue of their *particular* innate cognitive-mental talents and skills interacting with their environmental learning life-experiences, will be predisposed to, interested in, emphasize, and express their own *unique* pattern of *greatly differing* and *varied* knowledge and meaning contents and ways of expression. In general then, as One's expanding developmental consciousness pattern of compound personal-egoic *mental-cognitive* self continues, always, and as best you can, study, learn, listen, observe, experience, interpret, discuss, and share with others the *full spectrum* of Knowledge and Meaning which exists *within* Beauty, Truth and Goodness.

One's Transcendence of Separate Subject-Versus-Object Polarity-Duality

The *complete* transcendence, but also inclusion from perspective of such transcendence, of separate *subject versus object* polarity-duality mind consciousness is a *critical* hallmark of Awakening to Enlightenment. That is, You now Realize that, in Truth, You *are* the World; that, in Fact, You are the Kosmos Itself, of *all* worlds and universes, and Beyond. You are at once *both* subject and object (and neither also), since the *delusion* of *separate* subject-versus-object polarity-duality is now *utterly* transcended. And with *separate subject-object* consciousness transcendence, the *other-ness* and *separate-self-sense* of compound pre-personal self, personal-egoic self, and conditioned social-cultural self realities *no longer* arise or occur in Consciousness. This, of course, is because this delusional otherness and separate subject-versus-object *basis* for the functioning of these three compound personal-egoic self realities of mind has been transcended but included. Note, however, if you're seeking as a interior *subject* entity (as an individual-self-sense compound personal-egoic self and bodymind-identity person) for an external *object* of "Enlightenment" to possess, then that is quite futile and meaningless, since You always and already *are* complete Enlightenment *Itself*.

Buddhism's Bodhisattva Vow

From the *relative reality* perspective of compound pre-personal, personal, and interpersonal conditioned social-cultural *individual-self-sense* consciousness, Onliness theory fully embraces Buddhism's Bodhisattva Vow of *absolutely refusing* Awakened Enlightenment for One's Self, until *all* Consciousness Beings and Entities have *fully* Realized Enlightenment Awakening. In this way,

I encourage You to also embrace this Bodhisattva Vow. But, of course, understand that, in *Truth,* the uncontracted Bliss-Divine Self You already always are *unreservedly* and *completely* is and includes, is in *no way* separate from or other-than, all Consciousness Beings and Entities. Thus, as completely *all* of this World's Consciousness Beings and Entities, You *are* always already *each* and *every* of the World's sufferings, agonies, miseries and despairs, as well as *each* and *every* of Its happinesses, ecstasies, serenities and blisses; You are, right here and now, *all* of Its sorrows, tears, joys and laughter, without exception.

Self is the Incandescent Radiance that Illuminates All Worlds

Nondual Self-as-Self Consciousness Reality, That transcendent Mind which *You* now are, is the *true* Knower that *cannot* be Known; It is the *true* Seer and Witness that *cannot* be Seen or Witnessed. It is *Am*, without a *second* or *other*. Self is the Incandescent Radiance that *Illuminates* all Worlds. It is You, Your very Self-as-Self. But you must *Awaken to, Remember, Realize* and *Confess* this *Luminous Reality* that You always and already are. No one can do This for You. And the gateless gate of Enlightenment Awakening is right here before You, in *plain Sight.* Remember, Nondual Self-as-Self Awakened Reality *cannot* be lost or found, It is *not* hidden or obscure, but rather is right now Yours to See, Acknowledge, Recognize and Realize. There is *no secret* to or about It; ordinary everyday Self *is* the Way.

Nondual Self-as-Self Reality Simply Is and Is-not, and Is Neither

This Luminous transcendent Self You now are, is the Way of *Liberation*. This Nondual Self-as-Self Awakened Realization is Supreme and Boundless *Freedom,* and is also Ultimate and Absolute *Responsibility.* Awakening to *transcendent* Self Reality is neither earned or sought, nor awarded or assigned. Self simply *Is,* and *Is-not*, and is *Neither*. Its *spontaneous* Freedom and Liberation are like the unspeakable *flowing movement* of branches and leaves high in the tree, waving in undulation on a summer breeze. *Here* is the final Timeless *Freedom. Here* is beginning less and endless

Uncreated *Liberation*.

Nondual Consciousness Self Realization *is* the Way of Descent of *immanent* Compassion, Care and Loving Kindness toward *all* Consciousness Beings and Entities, in *all* Worlds and Universes. In *every* moment, the *fierce* intensity, severity and pervasiveness of suffering, remorse, agony, pain, hopelessness and sorrow that *each* and *all* Consciousness Beings and Entities must bear and must endure is overwhelmingly *beyond* all compound personal-egoic self human comprehension. And this is true, even when considering only the suffering of earth-centered human beings. Yet such *vast* and *pervasive* suffering, pain and agony is *exactly* what is *required* to be comprehensively and specifically identified, confronted, and responded to, in Self's Descent of immanent Compassion; which Descent is *inherent* to One's Nondual Spirit-as-Spirit Consciousness Awakening and Realization.

There Can Be No Ascent of Wisdom Without the Descent of Compassion

Without the Descent of *immanent* Compassion there can be no *transcendent* Ascent of Wisdom and Truth; and thus, there can be no *Awakening* to transcendental Nondual Self-as-Self Consciousness Reality. In each and every moment, One needs to *Awaken to, Embody,* and *Embrace* the profound and pervasive depth of suffering, misery, agony and pain of each and every Consciousness Being and Entity, with and through Compassion, Sacrifice, Care, Generosity and Loving Kindness. And, in this way, reduce or eliminate Others' suffering, through realizing, identifying, confronting, responding to, and directly addressing such suffering, misery, agony and pain. With *gratitude* and *appreciation* for this opportunity, You can thus devotionally *respond to* and *serve* Others in this way. And, *first*, always asks yourself, and carefully inquire into, this question: What direct or indirect role might I have played, what is my possible personal-individual self and societal-cultural self *contribution*, in the acceptance or promotion of other Consciousness Beings' and Entities' despondence, suffering, misery, agony and pain?

Within the daily consciousness of Your pre-egoic, personal-egoic and conditioned social-cultural compound self realities of mind, take *every* opportunity to *respond* and *act* with Loving Kindness and Compassion toward *each* Consciousness Being and Entity that You encounter, who may be or is in confusion, pain, suffering, or despondence, and thus lessen or eliminate that Being's or Entity's suffering, despondence, confusion and pain. As much as possible, depending on the *extent* to which You are embedded *in,* and identify *with,* the separate subject-object polarity-duality of pre-personal, egocentric-personal, and conditioned interpersonal social-cultural *compound* self and consciousness realities, do the *best* You can to *empathize* and *act* with Loving Kindness, Devotion and Compassion toward Others. And in this way, lessen the suffering of Conscious Beings and Entities that You daily encounter. Please also understand, that You need to be *patient* with Yourself, and to extend Loving Kindness and Compassion toward Yourself and Your own pre-egoic, egoic, and conditioned social-cultural compound self's suffering, confusion, despondence, anxiety and pain.

Witness Your Pre-egoic, Egoic, and Conditioned Cultural Self-contracted Functioning

In the course of Your spiritual development-evolution, you need to carefully *observe, witness,* and *directly acknowledge* the exact nature and dimensions of your moment-to-moment *self contracted* and *narcissistic* pre-personal self, personal-egoic self, and conditioned social-cultural compound self actions and functioning. More specifically, from a psychosocial-emotional wellbeing point of view, you need to come to consciously *see, acknowledge, understand, embrace* and *reintegrate* any and all of your own denied, projected, suppressed, repressed and alienated psychosocial-emotional problematic *shadow* dimensions. That is, reintegrate these *into* and *within* your three *interrelated* pre-personal, personal-egoic and conditioned social-cultural *compound* and *relative* self realities of consciousness.

So as to be fully accessible to *transpersonal* Awakening and Transformation, predominant-exclusive and self-contracted compound pre-egoic pre-personal self, personal-egoic self, as well as conditioned social-cultural self of *personal* identity and mind need to develop-evolve toward truthfulness, openness, wholeness, transparency, and thus *maturity*. This will facilitate One's *transpersonal* Realization of Open, Liberated, Spontaneous and Uncontracted *Trans-pre-egoic, Trans-egoic* and *Trans-conditioned social-cultural* Revelation and Insight into, and thus transcendence but inclusion of, these three relative and conditional interrelated self realities of consciousness. The difficult developmental-evolutionary *ordeal* involved in this numinous *Transformational Emergence* is almost always pre-personally pre-egoically, personally-egoically, and conditioned socially-culturally *profoundly* disruptive, painful and prolonged.

One's Relative Separate Subject-Object Singular Perspectival Self-Sense Realities

The *pre-transcendental* consciousness of *conditional* compound pre-personal self, personal-egoic self, and embedded-conditioned social-cultural self do not function separately from one another, but instead intensively *interact* and *overlap* (compound) with one another. These three *limited* and *self-constricted* compound self realities have both conscious and subconscious dimensions and domains. They all function as polarized *separate* subject-versus-object *singular perspectival* consciousness realities of mind. That is, these *separate-self-sense* relative and conditioned compound self realities see, interpret and comprehend manifest Form Reality from a *singular-specific* consciousness perspective, at any given moment of their developmental-evolutionary existence.

Self of Nondual Consciousness Intuitively Comprehends All Perspectives, All At Once

Beyond (transcending but including) these separate-self-sense polarized subject-object compound self realities of consciousness (i.e., beyond the conditioned and conditional delusion of polarity-duality's subject-versus-object separate-self-sense), *transcendentally* Awakened Nondual Self-as-Self *Intuitively Comprehends* and *Understands* all relative singular perspectives, all at once. That is, Nondual Self transcendent Consciousness is *Trans-perspectival*, in that It utterly *transcends* (but includes within such transcendence) the predominant-exclusive *singular* perspectival consciousness of compound personal-egoic self. In so doing, it Intuitively Recognizes, Realizes and Comprehends, *all* such relative consciousness perspectives *at once,* within this Trans-perspectival Consciousness Awakening.

Thus, the Mind Consciousness of Nondual Self-as-Self Reality, which You *truly* and *completely* are, is *not* restricted to a predominantly-exclusively *specific-singular* consciousness perspective at any given point (is not limited to *one* perspective only at any given moment), but *Intuitively* Comprehends and Understands the relative singular consciousness perspectives of *all* Consciousness Beings and Entities at once. Please understand that this *Inherent* Intuitive Consciousness of all-inclusive *Trans-perspectival Self* is always, already Your own *Innate* Nature and Condition.

In this way, what gradually and progressively Awakens within One, throughout the developmental realm-wave of Causal Holistence Consciousness, is this Intuitive *Trans-perspectival* Recognition and Realization Understanding of *all* Consciousness Beings' and Entities' singular perspectives, and *all at once*. However, by this, I am not implying that such an Awakened Being would possess specific and detailed knowledge of each Being's or Entity's relative and conditional singular-perspective perception and content of the moment. This broader and deeper transcendent Recognition and Realization Insight is a trans-mental, trans-egoic and transpersonal trans-perspectival Comprehension, and not a mental, egoic and personal singular-perspective relative recognition and realization insight comprehension.

Do Not Be a Follower of Me, Or of My Particular Way of Awakening

Beloved, You cannot, and should not try to, be a *follower* of Me or of My *specific* personal and particular Way of Awakening to Nondual Self Realization Consciousness. But rather, be an *innovator* and *creator* of Your *own* singular and unique Way of Awakening. I can only function as a spiritual Teacher and Guide to You, but that is all. Also, what I speak of here to You must *not* be interpreted and understood in a *dogmatized* or *literal-concrete* sense or way. Rather, the *interpreted meaning* of what I say needs to be subtlety and mindfully *Intuited* and *Understood* within a contextual *metaphoric-allegoric-poetic* Way of Comprehending. Please *do not* suppose or consider that I am a *leader* to be followed, to have followers, and *do not* literalize or concretize Your interpreted Meanings and Implications of what I say to You. And *certainly*, do not make of me an idol, god or cult. I neither *have* nor *hold* power, position, or importance.

I Speak to You from the Pre-transcendental Perspective of Vision-Logic Consciousness

What I tell You here is *necessarily* symbolically conveyed from the *pre-transcendental* perspective of advanced vision-logic consciousness, which is still primarily directed by pre-egoic, personal-egoic, and embedded-conditioned social-cultural-historical compound self realities of mind consciousness. In this way, the content of this narrative will *necessarily*, and to some *significant* extent, reflect and express my own *pre-personal* and *personal* bodymind-temporal self dimensionality, as well as my conditioned social-cultural, environmental and historical-era *contextual* self awareness and experience dimensionality. Thus, to the extent that I reflect, and thus express, these three *relative, self-contracted* and *conditional* compound personal-egoic self realities of consciousness, always keep in mind that I am an all too *fallible* and *mortal* human being, who lived a quite common co-created contextual earth-centered temporal life.

Use Your Trans-logical Intuitive Insight to Interpret What I Say to You

In Interpreting the deep-structure *transcendental* Meaning of what I say to You here, You need to carefully Recognize and *Distinguish* the content of my *singular perspectival* pre-personal,

personal-egoic and conditioned social-cultural-historical contextual compound bodymind self expression, *from* the Content of My *Trans-perspectival* Nondual Self-as-Self transpersonal, trans-egoic, trans-bodymind, trans-mental, trans-social-cultural, trans-contextual *omnipresent transcendent* Consciousness Expression, that I here Confess. *Trans-logical Intuitive Insight* application, through a *metaphoric-allegoric-poetic* Way of Knowing and Comprehending, will *help* You in such Recognition, Interpretation and Distinction.

To One's Compound Personal-Egoic Self, My Words Sound Grandiose and Strange

Interpret and Understand what the *infinite* and *eternal* Self *I Am* is Saying to You here, but Comprehend this from and through that transpersonal, trans-logical and trans-rational *Intuitive* Universal Heart and World-Soul that is *with* and *of* You always. To One's compound personal-egoic self, My Words sound grandiose and strange. However, it is *through* these *Intuitively* Interpreted and Comprehended Words that I transpersonally speak *directly* to the *Supreme Self* Nature and Condition that You are, to this Bliss-Divine Nondual Self Identity You are, will *always* be and have *ever* been. Listen to and *Hear* these Words, for They tell You of an *Awakening Way* of Spirit; they speak of Self-as-Self Nondual Consciousness Enlightenment. Acknowledge and Remember the deep and central Meaning of these Words, so that You come to cognitively *fully* Understand this *Awakened Consciousness Self-as-Self Reality.* This Luminous Awakened Self You now are, that I hereby attempt in language to symbolically imply, intimate and convey to You. Apply and Act upon these Words, as They *accord* and *relate to* Your own *unique* Path of transcendent Self Awakening. In this Way, then, *Become* the Bliss-Divine Self Reality that, in Truth, you always already are.

In Gratitude and Joy, Serve and Live with Care and Compassion for All Beings

Beloved, in gratitude and joy for this opportunity, devotionally *serve* and *live* with and through *Compassion* for *each* and *all*

Consciousness Beings and Entities. As best you can, initiate, respond and act in the moment-by-moment relative consciousness of your compound personal-egoic self's *everyday* life, so as to lessen and eliminate the suffering, fear, pain, confusion, agony, strife and struggles of *each* Consciousness Being and Entity that you encounter. To the greatest extent that you can, respond in, through and with *loving kindness*, *sacrifice*, *care* and *generosity,* by openly and unreservedly sharing your skills and knowledge in relationship with so called "other" Beings and Entities of Consciousness (as in *relative* mind of separate subject-object "otherness" perspective), so as to lessen or eliminate "their" suffering. As indicated, *This* is the Way of *Universal* Nondual Self-as-Self *Remembrance* and *Realization.*

The Ebb and Flow Complementarity of Kosmic Feminine and Masculine Expression

In Onliness theory, the knowledge, perspectives, values, insights, agency and actions of Kosmic Feminine versus Kosmic Masculine Communion, Wisdom, Compassion and Realization, although distinctly *contrastive* Visions from one another, are *always* of *equal* and *complementary* Relevance, Influence and Importance. These two Yin and Yang Kosmic *universal* principles of Feminine and Masculine Vision, Influence, and Revelation comprise a *fundamental* holon-polarity-within-unity in Onliness. And as Unity, They are two Sides or Faces of *one* and the *same* Mind of transcendental Bliss-Divine Self Reality. Each Face contrastively defines, embraces, contains and is contained within the Other. In One's (male or female person's) spiritual integral life practice, it is *so* important that there occurs an *equal* and *balanced* emphasis, an *integral complementarity,* in the ebb and flow of Kosmic Feminine and Masculine Expression, so that neither is *consistently* predominant-exclusive.

Nameless Uncreated Emptiness is Your Innate and Native Nature and Condition

In Your meditation, *open up* to the Silence of Emptiness. *Release* unto, and *rest* within, trans-conditional and uncontracted Silent

Emptiness. In meditation, when mind wanders let go of mental chatter and let attention return to Emptiness. Let go of rehearsing and rehashing pre-egoic, personal-ego, and conditioned social-cultural compound consciousness imagery and mentality, and return to boundless and timeless Emptiness Awareness and Experience. Radiant Emptiness is Your *native* Nature and Condition. This Bliss-Divine Nondual Self of transcendent Silence and Emptiness *is* All and None, and is also Neither; It is *ultimately* That which is *Nameless* and *Unknowable*.

One's Illumination of Relative Inward-Turning Self Remembrance and Recognition

The *radical* spiritual Transformation I speak of here almost always, at least for earth-centered human beings, requires a profound and devotional so called *Inward Turning* (in Truth, of course, Self has *no* Inward or Outward Reality). Transcendent Self Awakening will require a critically deep, and often painful, degree of *interior* Insight and Understanding, which will necessarily involve a great deal of pre-personal, personal-egoic, and conditioned social-cultural compound self reality witnessing, struggle, turmoil, confusion and frustration. But there will also be *profound* Illuminations of Serenity, Joy and Bliss in this relative Inward-Turning Self Remembrance and Recognition. In such Turning Inward, You will become Aware of, Experience, and will need to Endure, *severe* relative-self personal, social-cultural, emotional, and mental isolation, loss and loneliness. This *sustained* Ordeal and Revelation is one aspect in the *death*, the transcendence but inclusion within such transcendence, of *predominant-exclusive* and *contingent* pre-personal, personal-egoic, and conditioned social-cultural compound self reality and consciousness.

Disidentifying with One's Pre-Egoic, Egoic, and Conditioned-Cultural Self Realities

In this Inward Turning *Odyssey* and *Insight,* You will encounter and confront the *narcissistic, separatistic* and *isolative* nature and condition of predominant-exclusive pre-personal, personal-egoic, and conditioned social-cultural compound self and consciousness.

You will begin to *See* and *Comprehend* the *severe* limits, yet personal functional importance, of these relative and constricted compound self realities of mind. You will come to progressively Realize the origins, history, and process of your deep identity *with* and *as* this *bounded* and *superficial* compound personal-egoic mind of self, as well as Your embedded subconscious clinging and attachment to it. And ultimately, You will come to Recognize the *Means-whereby* of Your dis-identification with and as, Your transcendence but inclusion of, this *surface* and *self-contracted* compound personal-egoic self and consciousness.

One's Life Practice Needs To Be Multi-dimensional and "Otherness" Inclusive

Beyond interior mindful and meditative *relative* Inward Turning, One's spiritual integral life practice needs to be *multi-dimensional* and *"otherness"* inclusive; it needs to include *all* of the dimensions of so called "external" manifest Form Reality. Thus, in addition to this *Inward Turning,* Your spiritual life practice needs to *embrace* and actively *participate in* a so called *Outward Turning* of Mindful, Discerning and Compassionate Awareness and Experience; one that occurs *within* the social-cultural-environmental *"outer"* contextual world. What is required, is a *social-cultural-environmental* relative Outward Turning of *deepening* inquiry, recognition, understanding, and interactive participation-involvement within this contextual social-cultural-environmental "external" world.

As best You can, *Realize* and *Manifest* such participatory, interactive and committed Outward Turning *within* and *through* your spiritual integral life practice. Realize and Manifest this Outward Turning through *both* the *transcendent* Wisdom, Truth and Intuition, as well as the *immanent* Compassion, Care and Loving Kindness that, in Fact, You truly are. Within One's everyday integral life practice, carefully *observe* and *monitor* your own narcissistic fear-based and desire-based self-contraction, evasion, and withdrawal; *witness* these common conditioned habits of response, which are *central* to the functioning of predominant-exclusive pre-personal, personal-egoic, and conditioned social-cultural compound *pre-transcendental consciousness* self realities.

Also understand, that via the predominant-exclusive functioning of one's pre-personal, personal-egoic, and conditioned social-cultural compound self of mind consciousness, it is *absurdly easy* to be deluded, betrayed, distracted, and thus side-tracked, during and over the unfolding developmental course of One's Nondual Self-as-Self Consciousness Awakening and Realization. Indeed, as fallible human beings, we are the easiest and most gullible to be fooled *by ourselves* in this way, through *our own* self-deluded, distorted and self-contracted perceptions and conceptions, which derive from the functioning of this narcissistic compound personal-egoic self and mind of consciousness.

In Your spiritual life practice you will, at times, be *frustrated* and *impatient,* and will want to look for short-cuts, and less challenging and disruptive questions, answers and solutions, but there *are* none. At times, you will be *deeply* disheartened and discouraged, and will want to superficialize, turn away from, and even abandon your spiritual integral life practice, but you must *not*. Such transient conditional *emotional moods* of compound pre-personal, personal-egoic and conditioned social-cultural self and consciousness are of *no* important consequence, and need only to be noted, acknowledge and turned aside. Instead, *Walk On.*

Consciously Release Pre-Egoic, Egoic and Cultural Self-sense Identity and Attachment

Awakening to Nondual Consciousness Realization *necessarily* involves the conscious *surrender* and *abandonment* of predominant-exclusive pre-personal, personal-egoic and conditioned social-cultural compound self identities and attachments. That is to say, One *consciously* and *intentionally* lets go of predominant-exclusive compound personal-egoic self identities, responses and expressions *as* these arise and occur in consciousness. In this way, One *completely* and *utterly* dis-identifies with, and is thus released from, these relative and conditional compound personal-egoic embedded self realities. And it is One's committed spiritual integral life practice *itself* that is the

Means-whereby of this transcendence but inclusion Realization, this *complete* negation and preservation (within such transcendent negation), of these three deeply rooted, overlapping and habitual predominant-exclusive compound personal-egoic self identities and modes of mind consciousness.

Certainly, One's so called *Outward Turning* involvement and participation, that I speak of here, must occur *within* the *moral* and *ethical* spiritual integral life practice context of World-centric and Kosmos-centric *transpersonal* Truth, Wisdom, Compassion, Loving Kindness, Devotion and Love toward *all* Consciousness Beings and Entities - from molecules to mammals, and beyond. Specifically, the three Pure Precepts of Zen Buddhism comprise one formulation of sound advice in this regard: (1) Do no harm, (2) Do good, (3) Live to benefit all beings.

I Am the Ragged Vagabond Who Has Nothing of Importance to Say

My Teachings *fundamentally* accord *with* and are *of* the fathomless, unspeakable Tao. These Teachings return, again and again, to this timeless uncreated *Wellspring* hidden in plain sight, to this apparently devious, veiled and mysterious Way or Tao, from which there is *no* possible deviation, veil or mystery. I Am the Old One who speaks of the Watercourse Way. I Am the ragged vagabond who has Nothing of importance to Say, and whose speech is filled with Emptiness. *I Am* Nondual Self-as-Self Awakening of Bliss-Divinity. And indeed, *so* are You. But do *not* make of me a frozen religious idol, *nor* make of my Teachings a religion.

In Meditation, Release and Open Consciousness To Intuitive Heart-centered Emptiness

In meditation, one approach to Silence and Emptiness Awareness is to *focus* Attention trans-mentally, so as to support and cultivate *trans-rational* Intuitive Heart-centered Consciousness. Allow such *Heart-centered Intuition* to Clarify, Guide and Direct You in pre-personal, personal-egoic, and conditioned social-cultural compound self of mind consciousness *surrender* and *release*. Let

Your Intuitive Heart Inform You in this Way. Within such Heart-centered meditation Mindfulness, *focus*, *open* and *release* Attention to deeper and deeper realm-waves of transcendent Mind Consciousness, so as to become Aware of, and directly Experience, the more Consciousness-Inclusive realm-waves of this Bliss-Divine Nondual Self Reality that You always already are.

Trans-mental Intuitive Heart-centered meditation can initially begin with focus of direct *experiential* attention *to* and *throughout* all of your body's interior and exterior sensations, including muscular and breathing sensations, but in *complete* inner silence - without either ideational rationalizing, judging, analyzing, or getting sleepy or drowsy-dreamy. As your bodily sensations occur, and are simply monitored moment-to-moment in this non-judgmental way, next attend to your moment-to-moment awareness and experience of *all* accompanying *emotional* impulses and feelings, but in *complete* inner silence - without ideational rationalizing, judging or analyzing. Continuously *Witness* what it is You do and what You say as compound personal-egoic self of mind and consciousness. Again, I would emphasize that *all* of this needs to occur *without* accompanying rational-mental thoughts, ideas, judgments, ruminations, visions or analyses of *either* these bodily sensations *or* emotional feelings.

In this *initial* stage of meditation, as you come to release and rest compound personal-egoic bodymind self's rational and ideational rumination and judgmental thoughts into the non-rational, non-ideational and non-judgmental bodily-sensation and emotional-feeling realm-waves of awareness and experience, progressively let these *also* pass. Let go of this, and turn attention to *deeper* and *deeper* Awareness and Experience of Silence and Emptiness. Progressively, let Your Awareness and Experience become open to, and rest Consciousness within, the trans-egoic, trans-mental and trans-rational *Serenity* and *Silence* of Emptiness, but *now* let this occur with *no* attention whatsoever to sensations, emotions, images, visions, thoughts, goals, plans, judgments, ruminations, analyses, or ideas. Just sit in Silence and Emptiness *only*, deeper and deeper. Just *That*.

This trans-rational, trans-mental *Intuitive Heart-centered* meditation is just one of *many* ways to encounter, release, and open transpersonal Consciousness toward deeper realm-waves of Radiant Emptiness. As mentioned, another meditation approach is through focusing one's attention *solely* on the *sensations* of breathing, so as to return Attention to the native Silence and Emptiness that is Your Home, and is What You truly are. But understand, that *none* of these meditation-contemplation approaches involve compound personal-egoic self's goal seeking, or efforts of attainment or achievement. In meditation, You always remain completely *alert* and *awake,* in still and silent *attentive waking consciousness.* And in *serene reflection* meditation, in particular, you sit zazen with eyes mostly open and in an erect seated posture, but *without* tension or strain. Sit so that your back and neck are straightly aligned, and with the sensation of the top and back of your head "pointing" toward the ceiling.

Interior-Subjective Meditation By Itself Cannot Transcend Cultural-Self Identity

As important as interior-subjective individual meditation is in One's spiritual integral life practice, it cannot, *by itself,* enable *full* Awakening to Nondual Self-as-Self Consciousness Realization, no matter how long or intently One meditates. As Ken Wilber has carefully pointed out, this is so, because the *content influences* of One's *conditioned* social-cultural self identity are significantly *hidden* from view of relative compound personal-egoic self's individual interior subjective (including meditative) consciousness. Thus, *because* individual interior subjective consciousness is importantly unconscious of, and thus unaware of, the content influences of this *deeply rooted* conditioned social-cultural self identity and consciousness, such hidden conditioned social-cultural content tends to *subconsciously* distort, color and betray the Truthfulness of One's interior subjective *meditative* content revelations. That is, One's *personal subconscious* conditioned social-cultural biases, based on culturally provincial, limited, and self-contracted knowledge and understanding, will *appear* in meditation to be True *transpersonal* Knowledge, Insight and

Understandings, but they are *not*.

And it is *through* One's sustained integral spiritual life practice that there ultimately emerges, *within* the Consciousness Awareness and Experience of the developmental realm-wave of Causal Holistence Realization (Figures 2, 3, 4, 5, 6 and 7), the Transformational *Potential* to Unveil and Reveal these *unconsciously* biased and distorted mental contents, which derive from *provincially* conditioned and conditional social-cultural compound self and consciousness. And thus, it is *through* this Silent Witnessing realm-wave of *primordial* Self's Consciousness Awakening that there emerges the *Means-whereby* to *See Through* (to transcend but include) the unconsciousness influential provincially-biased and distorted conditioned social-cultural content by which, within individual interior-subjective meditation, One is *unconsciously* betrayed and blinded to the *Trans-cultural* Truth that can be Revealed through such meditation.

One's Transcendence from Conditioned-Cultural To Trans-Cultural Self Identity

As suggested, this conditioned social-cultural compound self's *transcendence* but inclusion will developmentally occur through One's Transformational Consciousness Realization within the realm-wave of Causal Holistence Reality (see Figures 2, 3, 4, 6 and 7). More specifically, One's *unprecedented* boundless, formless and unmanifest Pure Witnessing Consciousness of *Silence* and *Emptiness,* within Causal Holistence's *primordial* Self Identity, progressively unveils and fully reveals (and thus transcends but includes) the previously subconscious and unconscious conditioned social-cultural compound self's illusionary *separate* subject-versus-object based and oriented, provincially biased, distorted, and ethnocentric content. Thus, in meditation, One's *transpersonal* Insight and Understanding are no longer blinded by the *limited* and *distorted* provincial and ethnocentric *subconscious* content biases of this separate subject-versus-object based conditioned social-cultural compound self of consciousness.

This transcendence (but inclusion within such transcendence) of *illusionary* polarity-duality based *separate* subject-versus-object pre-personal, personal-egoic, and conditioned social-cultural compound self identity and consciousness, is a *radical* Universal Transformation. Such a *profound* Consciousness Transformation occurs, then, *from* this compound personal-egoic self's polarized *separate* subject-object based provincial, bounded, contingent, self-contracted, and finite identity and consciousness *to* Nondual Self's Trans-polarity-duality (and thus Trans-separate-subject-versus-object) *Universally Realized* Trans-contingent, Uncontracted, Infinite, Trans-conditional, Trans-pre-personal, Trans-egoic, and Trans-conditioned social-cultural, and Trans-perspectival, Self Identity and Consciousness. Please understand that, in large part, these Consciousness Revelations and Transformations derive from One's *transcendence* but inclusion of polarity-duality's separate *subject-versus-object* identity and consciousness, which is so *basic* to the existence and functioning of the three compound personal-egoic self realities of mind and consciousness.

The unprecedented Awakening to this Kosmic-Universal *primordial* Consciousness of Self Identity is, within this developmental realm-wave, a *Revelation* and *Expression* of Your true Nature and Condition. It is thus within, and at the culmination of, Causal Holistence Consciousness, that One comes to Understand and Realize the distorting provincially biased and ethnocentric *subconscious* content influences of compound conditioned social-cultural consciousness and self upon the Truth of interior subjective meditation Insight and Clarity. Indeed, it is at the culmination of this realm-wave that the very foundational ground of polarity-duality consciousness (which, in turn, is the underlying basis of polarized separate-self-sense subject-versus-object consciousness, which, in turn, is the underlying basis for the existence and functioning of compound personal-egoic self and consciousness realities), is not itself Real, is a delusion, and is thus transcended, but included within such transcendence.

With this Revelation of the ultimate delusion of polarity-within-unity consciousness itself, with this final and complete death (transcendence but inclusion) of the last vestiges of polarity-duality consciousness, there thus occurs the death of its co-dependent polaric-based *separate* subject-versus-object consciousness subset. And with this, there necessarily occurs the death in Consciousness of separate subject-versus-object based separate-self-sense pre-egoic, egoic, and conditioned social-cultural compound self and consciousness realities. Now, like "a house of cards," these three illusionary relative and conditional realities of polarity-duality consciousness, and its derivatives of separate subject-versus-object consciousness and compound personal-egoic self realities of consciousness, collapse, and thus no longer arise or occur (are transcended but included within such transcendence) in the Awakened Consciousness of Nondual Self Reality. Within the *Absolute Reality* of Trans-perspectival Nondual Self Consciousness Awakening, all of these transient conditional, conditioned and relative personal-egoic-related self realities of mind and consciousness are thus Unveiled and fully Revealed as illusions, and so, in Reality, are of no particular significance or importance whatsoever.

Please understand that *all* of these *Universalized* Trans-perspectival, Trans-pre-personal, Trans-personal-egoic and Trans-conditioned social-cultural Identity *Revelations* occur through One's transcendent *primordial* Self's *Silent Witnessing* of formless, boundless and unmanifest Consciousness Awakening, which occurs at the culmination of Causal Holistence realm-wave Reality - *if* all goes evolutionarily-developmentally well. In relation to *all* of these Transformational Awakenings, note that, *beyond* One's formal practice time in meditation, a Consciousness Being and Entity within this *Awakened Emptiness* of Causal Holistence Consciousness, *remains* in this Vigilant, Mindful and Meditative *Pure Witnessing* Awareness and Experiential State for virtually *all* of One's waking hours, day in and day out.

One's Transcendence of Separate Subject-Object Polarity-Duality Consciousness

In this way, it is with One's transpersonal Recognition and Realization within, and at the culmination of, Causal Holistence, that the *ultimate illusion* of polarity-within-unity Consciousness is *transcended,* but included within such transcendence. Thus, the Consciousness of *polarity-within-unity,* as well as *duality* - which is polarity without inherent unity, no longer arises or occurs in Consciousness (see Figures 2, 3, 4, 5, and 7).

In turn, in Onliness theory, it is asserted that relative mind's *polarity-based* separate subject-versus-object self and consciousness gives rise to, is the *basic* support and functional process of, predominant-exclusive pre-personal, personal-egoic, and conditioned social-cultural compound self realities. And without the *delusion* of separate-self-sense *subject-versus-object* polarity-duality consciousness and functioning, neither predominant-exclusive pre-personal, nor personal-egoic, nor conditioned social-cultural compound self realities of consciousness can any longer arise or occur in Consciousness. Thus, these three compound personal-egoic self realities of mind are *all* transcended, but included within this transcendence. For the first time then, One's polarized *separate* subject-versus-object consciousness illusions of an interior-subjective separate-self-sense "I" *versus* an exterior-objective *separately existing* being, object or entity of other and otherness (I-me-my *versus* they-that-it) is negated and preserved.

With this developmental realm-wave culmination then, You now Realize that, in Truth, You are *All* and *Every, beyond* the isolation and separateness of polarity-duality consciousness illusion; that Mind of *Nondual* Self-as-Self Reality *is only*, is without a second or opposite, and, in Fact, is *both* one and not one. That such *boundless* and *causeless* Enlightenment Awakened Self has no exterior versus interior boundaries, no external versus internal polarity-duality, no outside versus inside Reality. Indeed, this Self You always already are, has and is *no other-ness*, and *no* separateness whatsoever. And since, in Truth, there is no otherness or separateness of or about You, since, in Reality, You are All and Each and Every, what is this "other" that exists for You to desire, or to fear?

One's Realized Transformation from World-Soul to Universal Spirit Consciousness

Figure 1 visually symbolizes the three final human and human-like Beings' holon-polarity-within-unity realm-waves that culminate in the *initial* transcendence but inclusion, the initial stages of the collapse, dissolution and ultimately death, of *manifest* polarity-within-unity Consciousness *itself;* which collapse and death of its last *unmanifest* Consciousness vestiges finally and fully occurs at the culmination of Causal Holistence Consciousness. With cross-referencing *from* Figure 1 *to* Figures 4 and 6, the two smallest inner rings of Figure 1 symbolize the *universive* Subtle Prim-istence holon-polarity-within-unity of: *Pan-gnostic Existence Consciousness* (the cross-hatched ring) which, for *human* and *human-like* Beings, is their predispositional realm-wave (as explained in my previous books), versus *Trans-gnostic Existence Consciousness* (the blank smallest ring).

For human and human-like Beings, the two mid-sized rings symbolize the *supreme* Subtle Prim-istence holon-polarity-within-unity of: *Existence Being Consciousness* (diagonal-line mid-size ring), versus *Transexistence Being Consciousness* (blank mid-sized ring of Figure 1). For *all* Consciousness Beings and Entities, the two largest terminal rings symbolize *absolute* Subtle Holistent Prim-istence's *final* holon-polarity-within-unity of: *Being Consciousness* (diagonal-line largest ring), versus *Nonbeing Consciousness* (blank largest ring). And it is the *transpersonally* Realized Resolution and Synthesis of the holon-polarity-within-unity of Being *versus* Nonbeing Consciousness, that *initially* precipitates the complete and total *transcendence* but inclusion, negation and preservation, of polarity-within-unity (as well as duality) Consciousness *itself.* And thus, initiates the Emergence *from* World-Soul Self *to* Universal Spirit's *primordial* Self of Causal Holistence Consciousness.

In Figure 1, then, it is this *final* Being versus Nonbeing Consciousness holon-polarity-with-unity's (the two largest rings) *Transformational* Insight and Revelation (which *transcend* but include *all* previous (lower) holon-polarity-within-unity realm-waves of Consciousness), that functions as a *transitional* bridge *from* developmental-evolutionary World-Soul Consciousness *to* Universal Spirit Consciousness Realization. That is, Transformation *from* the *manifest* Consciousness Reality of *absolute* Subtle Holistent Prim-istence's *World Soul* Consciousness *to* the *unmanifest, formless* and *boundless* Reality Consciousness of Causal Holistence's *Universal Spirit* Consciousness.

For this *transitional* World-Soul *to* Universal Spirit *bridging* reason, the *"holon-polarity-"* dimension of Being versus Nonbeing *manifest* Consciousness Reality (the two largest solid-line rings of Figure 1) are symbolized in solid-line format, but the *"within-unity"* dimension of this *ultimate* and *terminal* holon-polarity-within-unity (the inclusive largest dashed-line ring) is symbolized in dashed-lines, because it partially belongs to, it symbolizes the *Emergent Recognition* of, the boundless, formless and *unmanifest* Consciousness of Causal Holistence Reality's *Universal Spirit* Awakening, which *transcends* but includes *all* polarity-within-unity and duality Consciousness.

Develop Courage to Effectively Ignore the Compound Ego World's Praise and Scorn

With *gratitude* and *humility*, and ever mindful of the subtle and not-so-subtle (but *always* all too easy) self delusions and ignorance involved in the very *real* pathologies of predominant-exclusive pre-egoic, egoic, and conditioned social-cultural self inflation and self importance, *embrace* and *manifest* Your developmentally *emergent* Consciousness of Nondual Self-as-Self Awakening, Remembrance and Realization. In this regard, I would suggest that you pay very *limited, critical* and *cautious* attention to what other conditioned and conditional samsaric-based compound personal-ego self human Beings *want* and *expect* you to do, or be, or think, or believe, or behave, or say. Develop the transpersonal *Courage* to carefully consider, but most often predominantly ignore, *both* their relative-mind-based approval *and* disapproval, and to most often dismiss and effectively ignore *both* their transient moods of praise and scorn - their acceptance and their rejection. And in this way, Mindfully observe the importance and practice of *Silence,*

Equanimity, and especially *Solitude,* in Onliness Awakening.

With the *transcendence,* but inclusion within such transcendence, of predominant-exclusive pre-personal, personal-ego and conditioned social-cultural compound self identities and consciousness, and thus Realization of *Trans-conditioned-social-cultural, Trans-egoic* and *Trans-pre-egoic* Self Identity and Consciousness, there emerges and occurs a profound Mind Awakening of Compassion, Insight and Wisdom. However, from Onliness perspective, such transcendent Awakening *inherently* requires that, within Your social-cultural-economic-political efforts of active commitment and involvement, You abide by, supports and accommodates nonviolent, worldcentric and universally just, rational, compassionate, ethical, truthful and wise societal-culture-economic-political actions, norms, customs and laws. And that You seeks such relative social-cultural-economic-political actions, goals and aspirations through completely *democratically* based legal means and changes.

And if such legal-option means are just *not* possible, that You do not hesitate to *openly* and *nonviolently* protest, through civil disobedience and revolt. That is, You *actively* help to create *nonviolent* revolution against such provincial, non-consciousness-inclusive, anti-universal, non-rational, cruel, inhumane, unjust, violent, false, unwise, unethical and compassionless societal-cultural-political actions, norms, customs and laws. But, from Onliness perspective, it is finally *You* who must *decide, act upon,* and *bear consequent responsibility for* all of your relative and conditional consciousness reality assertions, judgments, actions and decisions. However, *accomplished* and *expressed* in the ways described above, these are, in my view, *actually* and *truly* acts of Compassion and Loving Kindness.

The Compassion of *nonviolent Truth Force* response and agency, when required within relative consciousness existence, is, in Onliness Awakening theory and perspective, of *central* importance in One's spiritual integral life practice. Coercion, cruelty and violence leads *only* and *endlessly* to still *greater* coercion, cruelty and violence. Trans-pre-egoically, Trans-egoically, and

Trans-conditioned-socially-culturally Self Mindful and Awake, respond within the context of a *Worldcentric* and *Kosmos-centric* Vision and Perspective in each and every moment. Understand that the *profundity* of Bliss-Divine Nondual Self-as-Self Realization is *fully* Present, and is Who You *truly* are in each and every moment. Beloved, do not forget What and Who You are. *In* and *through* Your spiritual integral life practice then, learn of, teach, embrace, employ and act within Beauty, Truth and Goodness, which is Your *innate* inherent Nature, Condition and Identity.

In Onliness, What Is the Sequence of Realm-Wave Transformations that Occurs?

In the *Way* of Consciousness Being and Entity *transcendental* Awakening, let Me highlight for You, from Onliness theory and perspective, a summary of the *necessary* and *sufficient* sequential developmental-evolutionary course of One's transcendent Ascent-Descent Consciousness of Nondual Self-as-Self Recognition, Remembrance and Realization. In this, I attempt to describe the broad transpersonal Nature and *required sequence* of a portion of the major *Transformational* Consciousness realm-wave and trans-realm-wave dimensions that You can expect to developmentally emerge and occur in such Self Awakening. These sequentially described Consciousness realm-waves, which comprise a major portion of Onliness theory and perspective, can serve as a generalized *cognitive background-source* of information and insight into the developmental course of Your own *unique* odyssey and ordeal of transcendental Nondual Self-as-Self Consciousness Remembrance and Realization.

One's Holon-Polarity of Experience-Awareness Consciousness Awakening

I'll start with One's developmental-evolutionary Realization of World Soul *Experience* and *Awareness,* which, for human and human-like Being, is of *fundamental* Psychic Pan-gnostic Existence (which, in turn, is itself of *fundamental* Psychic Multi-istence), as visualized in Figures 2, 3, 4, 5, 6 and 7. For human and human-like Beings then, the realm-wave of holon-pole transpersonal

Experience Consciousness is the transcendental *ontological* Realization of *fundamental* Psychic Pan-gnostic Existence Consciousness (see Figures 2, 3, 4, 5, 6 and 7). It is One's *direct* transpersonal *Experience* of the Nature of transcendent Being and Beingness. This *unmediated* transpersonal Consciousness worldspace is the *intuitive* Heart-Soul's *Unreflexive* and *Transfigurative* Experience *of* and *as* all Consciousness Beings and Entities (which includes *all* of Reality Itself). This *World-Soul Experience* holon-pole manifests Itself *through* and *as* the *creative power* of transpersonal Ascent-Descent of Spirit or Self in the World. *Experience* is the *apparent transparency* Realization of One's Bliss-Divine World-Soul transcendent Consciousness Identity with and as *all* of Reality.

Conversely, for human and human-like Beings, the realm-wave of holon-pole transpersonal *Awareness* Consciousness is the transcendental *epistemological* Realization of *fundamental* Psychic Pan-gnostic Existence Consciousness (see Figures 2, 3, 4, 5, 6 and 7). It is One's *direct* transpersonal *Awareness* of the Nature of transcendent Knowledge and Knowingness. This *unmediated* transpersonal Consciousness worldspace is the *intuitive* Mind-Psyche's *Reflexive* and *Configurative* Awareness *of* and *as* all Consciousness Beings and Entities (which includes *all* of Reality Itself). This *World-Soul Awareness* holon-pole manifests Itself *through* and *as* the *productive vision* of transpersonal Ascent-Descent of Spirit or Self in the World. Awareness is the *transparent apparency* Realization of One's Bliss-Divine World-Soul transcendent Consciousness Identity with and as *all* of Reality.

The resultant co-arising and co-evolving *Experience-Awareness* holon-polarity-with-unity transcendent Consciousness that interactively emerges from these two holon-poles is, for human and human-like Beings, the *central* and *supreme* holon-polarity-within-unity of *fundamental* Psychic Pan-gnostic Existence Consciousness (see Figures 2, 3, 4, 5, 6 and 7). And it is the spiritually mediating-facilitating effects and influence of this *supreme* Experience-Awareness Consciousness holon-polarity that, in its Realization, *transcends* but includes the spiritually mediating and facilitating influences of either holon-pole *Experience* or *Awareness* transpersonal Consciousness alone and individually. Also, of course, Experience-Awareness holon-polarity-with-unity Consciousness *transcends* but includes, negates and preserves, *all* Consciousness holon-pole and holon-polarities prior to or below it (see Figures 2, 3, 4, 6, and 7).

Progressive Realization of All Eight Diverse-Beings Reality Pathways of Awakening

In human and human-like Beings, it is the full transcendent *Insight into* and *Realization of* the above described Dimensional Realities of World-Soul holon-polar *Experience-Awareness* Consciousness, that ultimately *precipitates* the developmental-evolutionary transition *from* Psychic Pan-gnostic Existence Consciousness Realization (of Psychic Multi-istence Consciousness) *to* Realization of Subtle Prim-istence Consciousness (see Figures 2, 3, 4, 6 and 7). With the Awareness and Experiential Emergence of *universive* Subtle Prim-istence Consciousness there occurs an initial Transformational convergence, whereby One *begins* to progressively transpersonally Experience, and become Aware of, the various Reality Pathways of Consciousness that occur *outside of* One's own human and human-like *predisposed* native *diverse-beings* Reality Pathway of transpersonal *Pan-gnostic Existence* Consciousness. That is to say, One begins to Comprehend the *dramatically* different natures and patterns of transcendent Consciousness Realization that occur *within* and *between* each of the other seven *diverse-beings* Reality Pathways of transcendent Consciousness Awakening: Trans-gnostic Existence, Pan-gnostic and Trans-gnostic Transexistence, Pan-gnostic and Trans-gnostic Istence, and Pan-gnostic and Trans-gnostic Antistence (see Figures 4, 6 and 7).

It is through the Transformational *convergence* within *universive* Subtle Prim-istence Consciousness, that the initial eight *separate* and *distinct diverse-beings* transcendent Reality Pathways of Psychic Multi-istence Consciousness *become* the eight *convergent diverse-beings* Reality Pathways of *universive* Subtle Prim-istence Consciousness. In this way, One begins to Realize a progressive *convergent-universalizing* Comprehension and Understanding of the *essential* Meanings of each of the other seven *diverse-beings* Reality Pathways of Consciousness Enlightenment. And, indeed, this converging Comprehension of the other seven *diverse-beings* Reality Pathways continues *throughout* the whole realm-wave of transcendental Subtle Prim-istence Consciousness. And finally at the developmental-evolutionary culmination of *absolute* Subtle Holistent Prim-istence, One's *Universal* Comprehension of the Meaning and Essence of *each* of the eight *convergent diverse-beings* Reality Pathways of Nondual Self-as-Self Consciousness Awakening are *unified, integrated* and *incorporated,* and thus become One and the same Pathway (see Figures 4, 6 and 7).

You Realize and Begin to Follow Your Natively Predisposed Way of Enlightenment

There also occurs a *second* major Transformation of transcendent Mind Awakening for *all* Consciousness Beings and Entities (including human, human-like and non-human) *through* and *within* this initial realm-wave emergence of *universive* Subtle Prim-istence Consciousness *from* the realm-wave Psychic Multi-istence Consciousness (see Figures 2, 3, 4, 6 and 7). This is an Awakening to the *eight* distinct *universal* Realization Modes or Ways of transcendent Enlightenment, that now *initially* occur for each and every Consciousness Being and Entity at this realm-wave of Consciousness. That is, from among these eight universal Modes of Enlightenment, One (human, human-like, and non-human) Awakens to and, for the first time, begins to *predominantly* follow, identify with, and develop One's own *specific* and *natively predisposed* Way or Mode of Enlightenment, from among one of these eight Consciousness Awakening Modes.

In Onliness, the eight broad categories of these unique *Modes* of transcendent Enlightenment Awakening are: yin and yang *Am, Actlessness, Emptiness, Radiance, Awakening, Mystery, Mind*, and *Onliness* (see Figures 5 and 7). But, according to Onliness theory, it is *only* throughout One's transpersonal World-Soul Awakening within *universive* Subtle Prim-istence that the eight Ways or Modes of Enlightenment continue to diverge and diversify, indeed, even as the eight *convergent diverse-beings* Reality Pathways continue to *converge* and *synchronize*. Thereafter, within the realm-wave Ascent-Descent of both *supreme* Subtle Prim-istence and *absolute* Subtle Holistent Prim-istence Consciousness, *both* the eight *Modes* of Enlightenment Realization, as well as the eight *convergent diverse-beings* Reality Pathways, progressively, but *separately* and *independently*, converge, integrate, synchronize, and incorporate.

Beginning Illuminations of One's True Bliss-Divine Identity as Spirit Itself

It is through One's developmental-evolutionary transpersonal (trans-being and trans-entity) Awakenings *within* the broad realm-wave of Subtle Prim-istence Consciousness, that *World-Soul* Compassion, Wisdom and Communion are *fully* Remembered and Realized. Here, in Radiant interior transcendental *Illumination* and *Clarity of Vision*, Spirit or Self, for the first time, begins to *directly* Awaken to and Realize Its *True* and *Ultimate* Bliss-Divine Identity; not only as an *Expression* of Spirit, but as Spirit *Itself*. In Onliness theory, it is proposed that in all human and human-like developmental realm-waves of Consciousness, One manifests, expresses and employs such transcendent Awakening and Realization through *both* what may be called an interior-subjective *Inward Turning* and exterior-objective *Outward Turning* of Awareness and Experience, as previously described.

One's Balanced Equalization of Ascent of Wisdom with Descent of Compassion

The *culmination* and *ultimate* resolution-synthesis of *universive* Subtle Prim-istence Consciousness is marked by One's (human, human-like, and non-human) emergent developmental-evolutionary balanced and synchronous *equalization-integration* of Spirit's or Self's transcendent *Ascent* of Wisdom, *with* Its immanent *Descent* of Compassion. In this way, there occurs *neither* an overall excessive and predominant (unbalanced-unsynchronized) *Trans-gnostic* relative emphasis on Spirit's transcendental Ascent of Wisdom, *nor* an overall excessive and predominant (unbalanced-unsynchronized) *Pan-gnostic* relative emphasis on Spirit's immanent Descent of Compassion. In Onliness theory and perspective, One's *overall* balanced *equalization-integration-synchronization* in the Ascent-Descent of *Wisdom* and *Compassion* Remembrance and Realization is the *critical* worldspace Consciousness Transformation that *precipitates* One's transition *from*, One's transcendence but inclusion *of*, *universive* Subtle Prim-istence, *to* Realization of *supreme* Subtle Prim-istence transcendent Consciousness (see Figures 2, 3, 4, 6 and 7).

Within the realm-wave of *supreme* Subtle Prim-istence Consciousness, One now Manifests and Expresses an overall *balanced, synthesized* and *synchronized* equalization-integration of Self's Ascent-Descent of Wisdom and Compassion. Thus, there *now* emerges only *four,* rather than the previous *eight* Pan-gnostic or Trans-gnostic prefixed, *convergent diverse-beings* Reality Pathways of transcendent Consciousness: Antistence Nonbeing, Istence Nonbeing, Transexistence Being and Existence Being (see Figures 2, 3, 4, 6 and 7). In turn, these four are represented within *each* of the *eight* Modes of transcendent Enlightenment Realization. See this representation symbolized in the two outside yin and yang digrams of the pentagrams of *supreme* Subtle Prim-istence Consciousness, that symbolize (within these pentagrams) each of the eight yin-yang paired Modes of Enlightenment in Figure 5, and then compare these four digrams to each of the four digram symbols for the four *convergent diverse-beings* Reality Pathways of *supreme* Subtle Prim-istence in Figure 6.

The eight *universal* Ways or Modes of Enlightenment - Am, Actlessness, Radiance, Emptiness, Awakening, Mystery, Mind, and Onliness - continue to manifest, interact, evolve and unfold in each Consciousness Being and Entity, whereby, for any given Being or Entity, *one* of them still tends to be more or less predominant throughout *all* of the developmental realm-waves of Subtle Prim-istence Consciousness Realization. And this *predominant* Mode for each and every Consciousness Being and Entity (human, human-like and non-human) continues to be the *primary* influence in mediating-facilitating One's developmental-evolutionary transcendental Awakening.

Supreme Subtle Prim-istence Partially Reveals Being and Nonbeing Reality's Nature

It's *through* and *within* One's developmental realm-wave of *supreme* Subtle Prim-istence Consciousness that the *initial* Nature and Dimensions of *Being* and *Nonbeing* transcendent Consciousness emerge, and are first Recognized. From the advanced vision-logic point of view of Onliness theory, the realm-wave of Being is the *predominant* Consciousness Reality of transcendent *Form*, while the realm-wave of Nonbeing is the *predominant* Consciousness Reality of transcendent *Emptiness*. The Mind Consciousness worldspace of uncreated and eternal *Being* is the open and abundant *Fullness* of Self's or Spirit's Abyss of *ever changing* and *evolving* Form. The Mind Consciousness worldspace of uncreated and eternal *Nonbeing* is the open and abundant *Freedom* of Self's or Spirit's Abyss of *ever changeless* and *formless* Emptiness.

There is Being's *Is-ness* of transcendent Consciousness, Being's Consciousness *Apparency*. And there is Nonbeing's *Anti-Is-ness* or *Is-Not-ness* of transcendent Trans-consciousness, Nonbeing Trans-consciousness *Transparency*. In Nonbeing, the prefix "Trans-" in "Trans-consciousness" is intended to mean "beyond" Being Consciousness, but not, however, in any sense above or below It.

The holon-polarity-within-unity of Being-Nonbeing transcendent Consciousness Realization is the reason I initially called Onliness perspective an "Isantis (Is-Anti-Is) Tao" cosmology (Treon, 1989). In Onliness theory, *Existence* is transcendent Being's *universal* Form Apparency, while *Transexistence* is transcendent Being's *universal* Form of Emptiness Apparency. Likewise, *Antistence* is transcendent Nonbeing's *universal* Emptiness Transparency, while *Istence* is transcendent Nonbeing's *universal* Emptiness of Form Transparency. The "Taoist Process of Yin and Yang" image on the front cover of this book, visually illustrates these relationships; wherein yang *Antistence* is the large white area, yin-within-yang

Istence is the small black circle within this white area, yin *Existence* is the large black area, and yang-within-yin *Transexistence* is the small white circle within this black area.

Further Convergence-Comprehension of Others' Diverse-Beings Reality Pathways

For human, human-like, and non-human Consciousness Beings and Entities throughout the developmental-evolutionary realm-waves of both *supreme* Subtle Prim-istence and *absolute* Subtle Holistent Prim-istence Awakening, there progressively occurs a merging *Comprehension* of, and *Identification* with, the Consciousness Reality Pathways of other diverse Consciousness Beings and Entities. Compared to earth-centered human Beings of advanced transpersonal Consciousness developmental Realization, the Consciousness nature and character of other human, human-like, and non-human Beings and Entities, within other worlds and universes, has previously been of *opposingly different* and *strangely foreign* structural and functional *diverse-beings* Pathways of Enlightenment. That is, Pathways of what can be *broadly* defined as transcendent Awareness, Experience, Wisdom, Compassion, Communion, Knowledge, Comprehension, Expression, and Meaning.

Within broad Subtle Prim-istence transcendent Consciousness then, One's progressively inclusive-embracing and merging-integrating Awareness and Experience of the *deep* structure, meaning and nature of Others' *convergent diverse beings* Enlightenment Reality Pathways emerges and occurs for *each* Consciousness Beings and Entities. In this way, such progressive *Consciousness-inclusive* Awareness and Experience occurs within and between the four *convergent diverse-beings* transcendental Pathways of: Existence Being, Transexistence Being, Istence Nonbeing and Antistence Nonbeing (see Figures 4, 6 and 7). Recall that *each* of these four *convergent diverse beings* Reality Pathways of Awakening occurs and is symbolized within *each* of the *eight* Realization Mode realm-waves of Enlightenment (see Figures 3, 5 and 7).

For human, human-like and non-human Beings and Entities, the *culmination* and *ultimate* resolution-synthesis of *supreme* Subtle Prim-istence Awakening, and thus its *transcendence* but inclusion, is marked by One's *convergent diverse beings* Realization of *Existence Being's* and *Transexistence Being's* unified and common *Ground* and *Source* in transcendent Consciousness, which is the more Consciousness-inclusive and Expansive worldspace of *Being* Consciousness Itself. And likewise, this realm-wave of *supreme* Subtle Prim-istence Consciousness is transcended but included *through* One's *convergent diverse beings* Realization of *Antistence Nonbeing's* and *Istence Nonbeing's* unified and common *Ground* and *Source* in Consciousness, which is the more Consciousness-inclusive and Expansive worldspace of transcendent *Nonbeing* Consciousness Itself (see Figures 4 and 6).

Realization of the Final Holon-Poles and Holon-Polarity of Being and Nonbeing

In Onliness theory and perspective, Beings and Entities in spiritual development-evolution, just prior to the transcendence but inclusion of *supreme* Subtle Prim-istence Consciousness, *still continue* to be predominantly (but not exclusively) predisposed toward *either* Being *or* Nonbeing transcendent Awareness and Experience Realization. It is only with the realm-wave *onset* of *absolute* Subtle Holistent Prim-istence, that there initially emerges, in human, human-like and non-human Consciousness a profound Awakening to, and Realization of, the *equal, unitary* and *complementary* Consciousness Realities of *both* holon-pole Being and Nonbeing Consciousness Awakening (i.e., the progressive abandonment of One's primary *predisposition* toward either one or the other of these two holon-pole Ways for Consciousness Realization). And with this, there occurs the *initial* transcendent Awakening to the spiritual Power of Being-Nonbeing *holon-polarity-with-unity* Awareness and Experience Consciousness, which is *fully* Realized within *absolute* Subtle Holistent Prim-istence.

This transcendent Being-Nonbeing realm-wave Consciousness is the *ultimate* and *final* holon-polarity-within-unity of all *diverse beings* Reality Pathway holon-polarity-within-unities. Which is to say, *this* final holon-polarity-with-unity is the *most* Expansive and Consciousness-inclusive of *all* such previous holon-polarities. And, within One's *convergent diverse-beings* Consciousness Pathway, it is this *initial* and *preliminary Awakening* to the *equality, unity* and *complementarity* of both holon-pole Being and Nonbeing transcendent Realities, and with this, the *initial* Awakening to the *interactive, integrated* and *complementary Unity and Power* of Being-Nonbeing holon-polarity-within-unity Consciousness, that finally *precipitates* One's transition from *supreme* Subtle Prim-istence to *absolute* Subtle Holistent Prim-istence transcendent Consciousness (see Figures 2, 3, 4 and 6).

Recall that in Onliness, there are *sixteen* yin and yang quadragram-symbolized universal holon-pole *Modes* of Enlightenment that attempt to broadly describe *all* of the predominant Ways of transcendent Awakening and Realization, for *all* Consciousness Being and Entities (see Figures 5 and 7). In turn, these *sixteen* yin and yang holon-poles respectively comprise the *eight* distinct predispositional universal *Modes* of Enlightenment Awakening *holon-polarities.* Note that in this way, *Being* Consciousness (*yin* symbolized in Figures 6 and 7, and in the outside unigram of the eight *yin* Figure 5 quadragrams), and *Nonbeing* Consciousness (*yang* symbolized in Figures 6 and 7, and in the outside unigram of the eight *yang* Figure 5 quadragrams) find Expression in *each* of these eight Enlightenment Modes of: Am, Actlessness, Radiance, Emptiness, Awakening, Mystery, Mind, and Onliness (see Figure 5). And it is over the developmental course *of* this realm-wave of *absolute* Subtle Holistent Prim-istence Consciousness, that these two *convergent diverse-beings* Reality Pathway holon-poles of *Being* and *Nonbeing*, and, of course, their Being-Nonbeing holon-polarity-within-unity, *fully* emerge, and progressively manifest, interact, balance, synchronize, complement and converge in Consciousness.

Being's Ever-changing Fullness of Form Apparency and Nonbeing's Ever-changeless Freedom of Emptiness Transparency are Realized

Over the development-evolution of *absolute* Subtle Holistent

Prim-istence, the transcendent *Content* and *Nature* of One's *convergent diverse-beings* Reality Pathway, of predominantly *either* Being or Nonbeing Consciousness, continues to *converge* and *merge,* such that Being and Nonbeing Consciousness Realization become progressively more *Recognizable, Intelligible* and *Interpretable* to one another. In this way, there occurs in Consciousness Awakening a progressive synchronous *resolution-synthesis,* whereby One (human, human-like, and non-human) transcendently Comprehends, inclusively Realizes, and *equally* Identifies with, *both* the uncreated and eternal ever-evolving *Configurative Fullness* and *Apparency* of Being's ever-changing *Radiant Form,* as well as the uncreated and eternal non-evolving *Transfigurative Freedom* and *Transparency* of Nonbeing's ever-changeless *Radiant Emptiness.*

Thus, Being and Nonbeing Consciousness Realities are Remembered and Realized as the two holon-polar *Faces* or *Sides* of *One* and the *Same* transcendent Consciousness Reality of Self. And thus, the Realization: "Form *is* Emptiness, Emptiness *is* Form." Beloved, *all* of these postulated descriptions, presented here from Onliness theory and perspective, are simply advanced vision-logic pre-transcendental consciousness *conceptual* formulations of the nature and necessary sequence of the broad developmental transcendent Consciousness *realm-waves* of *Awakening* to this *Mind* of Nondual Self-as-Self Reality, that You always already are.

One's Original-Unique Predispositional Pattern in the Eight Enlightenment Ways

As suggested, as a function of One's (human, human-like, and non-human) *innate* temperament and environmental experiences, Onliness theory asserts that *each* Consciousness Being and Entity has an *original* and *unique* hierarchically arranged, but evolving, *pattern* of interactive *predispositions* within and between the *eight* holon-polar Ways or Modes of Consciousness Enlightenment. These predisposition initially emerges at the beginning of the developmental World-Soul realm-wave of *universive* Subtle Prim-istence Consciousness. Thus, within each Being and Entity, until the initial developmental realm-wave of *absolute* Subtle

Holistent Prim-istence Awakening, there exists a unique pattern of variously and unequally balanced *predispositional tendencies* among and between the holon-poles and holon-polarities of that Being's eight Ways or Modes of Enlightenment Awakening.

One's Progressive Transcendence but Inclusion of Polarity-Duality Consciousness

In Onliness theory, one of the developmental Transformational Consciousness *convergences* that is proposed to occur for *each* Being and Entity within *absolute* Subtle Holistent Prim-istence, over Its *initial* course, is the convergent merging-integration, to *complete* transcendence but inclusion, of One's *unequally* balanced holon-pole and holon-polarity *predispositional tendencies* between these *eight* Enlightenment Modes of Am, Actlessness, Radiance, Emptiness, Awakening, Mystery, Mind, and Onliness. In this way, all Comprehension, Manifestation and Expression of *each* of these eight holon-polar Modes become of *integrated, balanced* and *equal predispositional tendency* for each such Consciousness Being and Entity, but only at this *mid* realm-wave point of One's development within *absolute* Subtle Holistent Prim-istence.

And over the *final* developmental course of *absolute* Subtle Holistent Prim-istence Consciousness, there occurs, at its culmination, a convergent merging-integration to *complete* transcendence but inclusion of these eight *separately* occurring but equally balanced, holon-polar Modes of Enlightenment predispositional tendencies. At this developmental culmination, then, there emerges and occurs in Consciousness the effective transcendence but inclusion of *all eight* of these *separately* arising and occurring holon-polar Modes of Consciousness Realization, and thus, of course, the transcendence but inclusion of their *separately* arising and occurring sixteen yin and yang holon-pole Modes of Consciousness Awakening.

Similarly, the *other* convergent merging-integration of transcendent Consciousness that is proposed to occur for each Being and Entity within *absolute* Subtle Holistent Prim-istence, over its *initial* developmental course, is the *complete* transcendence but inclusion of One's *unequally balanced* predominant tendency toward the *convergent diverse-beings* holon-pole Reality Pathway of either *Being* or *Nonbeing* Consciousness Awakening. In this way, One's (human, human-like, and non-human's) Comprehension, Manifestation and Expression of *both* Being and Nonbeing transcendent Consciousness become of *integrated, balanced* and *equal* predispositional tendency for each Being and Entity, but only at this *mid* realm-wave developmental point of *absolute* Subtle Holistent Prim-istence Consciousness.

And over the *final* developmental course of realm-wave *absolute* Subtle Holistent Prim-istence Consciousness, there occurs, at its culmination, a convergent merging-integration to *complete* transcendence, but inclusion within such transcendence, of the two remaining *diverse-beings* Reality Pathways of the separately arising and occurring, but now equally balanced and integrated, holon-polar Being and Nonbeing Paths of Consciousness Realization. For human, human-like, and non-human Consciousness Beings and Entities, then, neither holon-pole Being nor Nonbeing Awareness and Experience will any longer arise or occur in Consciousness; nor, of course, will their of Being-Nonbeing holon-polarity-within-unity any longer arise or occur in Consciousness.

With this final developmentally Awakened transcendence but inclusion of *all* holon-polarity realm-waves of Consciousness, which occurs at the *culmination* of *absolute* Subtle Holistent Prim-istence Realization, polarity-within-unity *itself*, as well as duality (polarity only), no longer arises or occurs in Consciousness. Holon-pole and holon-polarity co-constructed realm-waves of Consciousness no longer emerge, manifest or exist in Consciousness, with the resolution and closure of these *final* holon-polar realm-waves. At the culmination, then, of *absolute* Subtle Holistent Prim-istence Consciousness, *both* One's *final* remaining *convergent diverse-beings* Reality Pathway realm-waves of *holon-polar* Being and Nonbeing transcendent Consciousness, *as well as* One's eight *holon-polar* realm-wave Modes of Enlightenment Awakening, of Am, Actlessness, Radiance, Emptiness, Awakening, Mystery, Mind, and Onliness, are utterly and completely *transcended* but included, *negated* and preserved (see Figures 2, 3, 4, 5 and 6).

One's Holon-Only Consciousness Becomes the Singular Vehicle of Awakening

No longer is *holonic-polaric* Consciousness manifest, no longer does holon-polar transcendent Realization emerge, occur and find expression in One's transcendent Consciousness. But, rather, a new *Holistent* Consciousness of *holon-only* transcendent Realization manifests and remains. *This* is now One's *singular* Vehicle or Way of transcendental Recognition, Remembrance and Awakening to Mind of Nondual Self-as-Self Reality. This holon-only Vehicle is now shared by *each* and *every* Consciousness Being and Entity at and beyond the developmental-evolutionary culmination and completion of *absolute* Subtle Holistent Prim-istence's realm-wave Consciousness.

One Awakens from World Soul to Universal Spirit in Causal Holistence Reality

In this way then, the *culmination* and *ultimate* resolution-synthesis of *absolute* Subtle Holistent Prim-istence Consciousness is marked by One's *Transformational Realization* of the *Nondual* holonic-only Nature, Identity and Unity of Causal Holistence Reality, of Causal Holistence Self, or Spirit. This new holonic-only Consciousness marks the emergence of developmental *trans-polaric* Causal Holistence Awakening. And thus, with this, there emerges One's corresponding Realization that the *seeming* and *apparent duality* and *polarity-within-unity* of Spirit is itself a co-constructed surface-structure mind *illusion*. And it is *this* more profound *Transformational* Remembrance and Realization that now *precipitates* One's transition *from* the *World Soul* Reality of holon-polar *absolute* Subtle Holistent Prim-istence Consciousness *to* the holon-only Reality of *Universal Spirit* Consciousness, which initially occurs within the Causal Holistence realm-wave of *primordial* Causal Arch-istence Consciousness (see Figures 2, 3, 4, 5, 6 and 7).

More specifically, with One's *complete* transcendence but inclusion of polarity-duality Consciousness, the two major holon-polar *convergent* dimensions of World Soul *absolute* Subtle Holistent Prim-istence (i.e., the *diverse-beings Reality Pathways* of Being and Nonbeing, and the *eight universal Modes* of Enlightenment Consciousness) are *themselves* transcended but included. In this way, there occurs in One a Transformational Consciousness *convergence-synthesis* Realization, a complete transcendence but inclusion, of *both* the final *convergent diverse-beings* holon-poles and holon-polarity Reality Pathway of *Being* and *Nonbeing* Consciousness, *and* the transcendence but inclusion of each and all of the *eight* holon-pole and holon-polarity universal Modes of Enlightenment Awakening - which, overall, are now integrated to include both yin-Being and yang-Nonbeing of *Am, Actlessness, Radiance, Emptiness, Awakening, Mystery, Mind,* and *Onliness* Consciosuness.

It is One's final Consciousness transcendence but inclusion of these *two* holon-polar based convergent World Soul dimensions (i.e., the eight Enlightenment *Modes* and the two *diverse beings* Enlightenment Reality Pathways) that *precipitates* the transition *from* transcendent *World Soul* Consciousness of *absolute* Subtle Holistent Prim-istence, *to* the transcendent *Universal Spirit* Consciousness of Causal Holistence Reality. Freed of the mind of polarity-within-unity and duality illusion, suddenly, and for the first time, One Intuitively and with great Clarity, *Sees* and *Understands, beyond* the mind of holon-polar Consciousness, the trans-polaric *singular Luminous Totality* of Self *as* uncreated Bliss-Divine Reality, *only* and *complete*.

One Initially Awakens to Trans-perspectival Consciousness in Causal Holistence

According to Onliness theory, it is within holon-only (no longer holon-polar) Causal Holistence Consciousness that the last shadow vestiges of One's *polarity-duality-based* separate subject-versus-object compound personal-egoic self and mind of consciousness, as well as One's corresponding inherency of polarity-duality based separate-self-sense *singular-perspectival* consciousness, are finally and completely transcended but included. With the transcendence (but inclusion within such transcendence) of these delusional *shadow vestiges* of polarity-duality based *isolated* separate-self-sense subject-versus-object consciousness, One's corresponding *isolated* separate-self-sense *singular-perspectival* consciousness perception no longer arises or occurs in Consciousness.

With this developmental transcendence-but-inclusion *Recognition* and *Realization* of the ultimate *illusion* of *holon-polar* (holon-pole and holon-polarity-duality) consciousness, with its innate singular-perspectival consciousness perception, there emerges in One's (human, human-like, and non-human) Awareness and Experience an initial *Intuitive Trans-perspectival* transcendental Consciousness Awakening. That is, *beyond* the ultimate illusion of polarity-duality consciousness, with its *limited, fragmentive* and *isolative* consciousness boundaries, One *initially,* and then *progressively*, Recognizes, Realizes and Comprehends *all* Consciousness Beings' and Entities' separate-self-sense singular perspectives, and all at once. However, this *Intuitive* Recognition and Realization Insight is a trans-mental, trans-egoic and transpersonal trans-perspectival Comprehension, and not a mental, egoic and personal singular-perspectival relative recognition and realization insight comprehension.

At the *culmination,* then, of developmental-evolutionary Causal Holistence Consciousness, there is, for You, *no* estrangement or otherness or separateness from *Anything* or *Anyone*. In this developmental realm-wave of Truth-consciousness, at its culmination, One (Self) *transcends,* but includes within such transcendence, all of One's compound personal-egoic self's *singular perspective* mind consciousness. In such Truth-consciousness, You now fully and completely *are* Each and All Expressions and Realizations of Nondual Self's Universal Consciousness. You are, in Fact, *each* and *every* Consciousness Being and Entity, without exception. And when, as Self, You *are* completely All and Each, You have *Intuitive Knowledge* of, and *Insight* into, All and Each. However, more completely, it should be said that You *are* All and Each, but also None.

Upon the completion of realm-wave Causal Holistence, with *all* remaining shadow vestiges of pre-personal, personal-egoic and conditioned social-cultural compound self and consciousness *completely* transcended but included, You now *fully* Awaken to this transcendental Causal Holistent *primordial* Consciousness of Bliss-Divinity truly You are. And it is this full and complete transcendent Realization, that finally precipitates Your transition *from* Causal Holistence realm-wave Consciousness *to* the trans-realm-wave *Ultimate Reality* of Nondual Self-as-Self Consciousness Awakening.

You are This Unmanifest Seer, In and Through which All of Manifest Reality Arises

Excluding any developmental-evolutionary spiritual pathology, One's (human, human-like, and non-human) developmental course, this immanent Descent of Compassion and transcendent Ascent of Wisdom, within *holon-only* Causal Holistence Consciousness includes: the initial *holon-only* realm-wave of *primordial* Causal Arch-istent Holistence, followed by the *holon-only* realm-wave of *primordial* Causal Omni-istent Holistence Consciousness (Figures 4, 6 and 7). Unique to *all* transcendental Recognition and Realization within realm-wave Causal Holistence Awakening is One's Silent and Mindful *Witnessing,* which is of formless, boundless and unmanifest transcendent Consciousness.

At the *center* this Awakening Mind of Causal Holistence Consciousness, is One's supreme *Silence* in Direct, Vigilant and Mindful *Witnessing of* and *as* this *primordial* Self of Fullness and Emptiness that, in Fact, You are. This is *primordial* Self's Witnessing *of* and *as* the *Seer, in* and *through* which *all* of the *impermanent* forms, processes and boundaries of *manifest* Reality arise, occur, and pass. And *You* are this Witnessing *primordial* Self of Causal Holistential transcendent Reality, this Silent Self or Spirit of formless, boundless and unmanifest Causal Holistence Consciousness. But understand, this Awakened *primordial* Self of Causal Holistence Consciousness is *not yet* fully Realized and Awakened Mind of Nondual Self-as-Self Reality.

One's Identity as Unmanifest, Boundless and Formless Trans-perspectival Self

Within the *holon-only* (no longer either holon-polarity-with-unity or duality) Consciousness of Causal Holistence's *primordial* Self, One *progressively* becomes Aware of and Experiences *profound* and *radical* transcendent Visions, Insights and Realizations of *Trans-perspectival* Awakening and Identify. With the emergence of Holistent *Universal Spirit* Consciousness, which marks the *transition* into the realm-wave of Causal Holistence, the *World Soul* Consciousness of Subtle Prim-istence and Psychic Multi-istence Awakening is *transcended* but included, negated and preserved. And it is the *full* Recognition and Realization of One's *Identity* with and *Reality* of and as unmanifest, boundless and formless Mind of *Trans-perspectival* Causal Holistent Self and Consciousness that is progressively *Revealed* within Causal Holistence (see Figures 2, 3, 4, 6 and 7).

One Realizes an Even More Inclusive Ascent of Wisdom and Descent of Compassion

One's *Transformative* Recognitions and Realizations of Consciousness that occur in this *Silence* of *Unbounded Witnessing* within Causal Holistence, are not merely mental abstractions, ideas or metaphors, but rather are *direct, immediate* and *profound* transcendental Awareness and Experiential Awakenings, *to* and *as* *primordial* Self, Spirit, Reality. And through these *unfolding* and *enfolding* Causal Holistence Awakenings, there Occurs, and is Revealed, an even *more* Consciousness Expansive and Inclusive transcendent *Ascent* of Spirit in Wisdom, and corresponding immanent *Descent* of Spirit through Compassion.

Transcending the Last Vestiges of Polarity-Within-Unity and Duality Consciousness

From Onliness perspective, *at least* for manifest human and human-like Beings, polarity-within-unity is an *innate* and *inherent* structure of much of pre-transcendent consciousness and transcendent Consciousness Reality. Because of this *polaric* centrality and inherency, Onliness theory asserts that the Consciousness of *manifest* human and human-like Beings (and possibly non-humans as well), especially within the early realm-wave stages of *unmanifest* Causal Holistence Consciousness, *includes* the *unmanifest* lingering "shadow," so to speak, of holon-polarity-within-unity and duality Consciousness.

Especially initially within Causal Holistence, One's transcendent Consciousness will include the *unmanifest,* but implicit, *vestige* Consciousness of holon-polarity-within-unity and duality. However, according to Onliness theory, the *explicit* or *fully expressed* manifestation of holon-polarity-within-unity and duality does *not* occur within the Silent and Mindful Witnessing of unmanifest, boundless and formless Consciousness, which characterizes and defines Causal Holistence Awakening.

The critical transcendence but inclusion *ordeal* for all human and human-like (and possibly non-human) Beings and Entities within Causal Holistence Reality, will involve and require the *complete* and *final* Resolution (transcendence but inclusion) of these last shadow vestiges or "remnants" of *polarity-within-unity* and *duality* Consciousness. These Consciousness vestiges include, among others, the *implicit* holon-polarity-within-unity of manifest-unmanifest itself, as well as form-formless, bounded-boundless, and *especially* vestiges of separate *subject-versus-object* polarity-duality (e.g., I and It, we and they, Seer and that which is Seen).

Beyond Separate Subject-Object Polarity Consciousness No Otherness Arises and Occurs

One's *transcendence but inclusion* of these polarity-within-unity and duality vestiges within Causal Holistence is *critical,* because polarity-duality consciousness is so *central* to the *separate subject-versus-object* polarity-duality which is at the *heart* of separate-self-sense *pre-personal, personal-egoic* and *conditioned social-cultural* compound self realities of mind and consciousness. Thus, with the *final* death (transcendence but inclusion) of this remaining implicit *separate subject-object* polarity-duality consciousness vestige, which, in turn, fundamentally underlies and supports the corresponding implicit vestiges of pre-personal self, personal-egoic self, and conditioned social-cultural self realities, these three realities of compound personal-egoic self reality will *no longer* arise or occur in Consciousness.

This *Liberating* Transformational Realization developmentally occurs at the *culmination* of Causal Holistence realm-wave Consciousness. With this, One now Realizes that there is *no* polarized otherness or separateness at all, no *separate* subject versus object, *of* or *as* the Truth-Consciousness that is Nondual Self-as-Self Reality; that One always and already *is* All and Each and Every, without exception. In this way, one's separate-self-sense *illusion* of polarized *separate* subject-versus-object consciousness now *completely* unwinds and unravels, and is no more.

As indicated, with One's *profound* Realization of the *illusion* of separate *subject-versus-object* consciousness polaric fragmentation, separate subject-object polarity-duality *no longer* at all arises or occurs in Consciousness. Now, *beyond* these vestige illusions, *without* this polaric separate subject-object "I-and-it" delusion, You *fully* Realize that You are *All* and *None,* always and already; that, in Reality, You *are* the World, but *also* transcend but include the World. And, in *This*, there is and occurs *no* externalness in Consciousness - *no* it, *no* object-ness, and *no* contrasting subject-ness, and thus *no* estrangement, no exclusion. There occurs neither interior subject nor exterior object, *no* separateness or otherness at all.

Partial *Recognition* of Nondual Self-as-Self within Causal Arch-istence Consciousness

One's developmental-evolutionary Consciousness of *primordial* Causal Arch-istent Holistence is, at its culmination, marked by the full and complete *Recognition* (but not full and complete *Realization*) of Bliss-Divine Nondual Spirit-as-Spirit Mind of Consciousness Awakening, this Onliness of ultimately *indefinable* and *inexpressible* Self Reality. However, within the transcendent

Consciousness unfolding of its initial *sub-realm-wave* of *primordial* Causal Arch-istence, there is Revealed only a *partial* and *incomplete Recognition* of Nondual Self-as-Self Reality (see Figures 2, 3, 4, 6, and 7).

Specifically, in One's *Awakening* within sub-realm-wave *primordial* Causal Arch-istence, there is *Revealed* a profound, but still partial and incomplete, transcendent Consciousness *trans-polaric Recognition* of the shadow vestige illusion of *polarity-within-unity* and *duality* Consciousness. And, in turn, *through* this profound, but incomplete, polaric consciousness transcendence but inclusion, there is correspondingly *Unveiled* and *Recognized* a partial and incomplete transcendence but inclusion of the shadow vestige illusion of polarity-duality's consequent separate *subject-versus-object* consciousness.

Consequently, and correspondingly, there now arises and occurs in Consciousness a more Insightful, but still partial and incomplete, *Recognition* of polarity-duality's perceived separate *subject-versus-object based* shadow vestiges of *pre-personal*, *personal-egoic* and *conditioned social-cultural* compound self realities and consciousness. And partially without (partially beyond) such separate *subject-versus-object* polaric consciousness, upon which compound personal-egoic self realities of consciousness are founded and established, these three contingent and relative compound personal-egoic self realities have only the partial and incomplete *grounding* of structure and function through which to operate, and thus they no longer can *fully* arise or occur in such partially trans-polaric Recognition Consciousness. Through this series of sequential transcendent Insights then, there is Unveiled a *Recognition*, though partial and incomplete, of One's Bliss-Divine Nondual Self of Consciousness Identity and Reality.

Full *Recognition* of Nondual Self-as-Self within Causal Anti-arch-istence Consciousness

It is One's emergent developmental Consciousness *Awakening* within sub-realm-wave *primordial* Causal Anti-arch-istence that marks the *full* and *complete* transcendent *Recognition* of

Bliss-Divine *Nondual* Self-as-Self Reality and Mind of Consciousness. That is, *Nondual Self* in the sense of being *neither* holon-polarity-within-unity or holon-only, *nor* not holon-polarity-within-unity or holon-only Consciousness, and also simultaneously both. With the *final* unfolding Consciousness Revelations within this second holon-only *sub-realm-wave* (of the larger realm-wave of *primordial* Causal Arch-istent Holistence), there emerges One's *full* and *complete* transcendent *Recognition* Awakening to Nondual Self of no-self Consciousness Identity and Mind Reality (see Figures 2, 3, 4, 6 and 7).

In this Way, there is *Revealed* an even more Consciousness Inclusive *trans-polaric Recognition* (transcendence but inclusion) of *all* remaining shadow vestige illusions of *polarity-within-unity* and *duality* Consciousness. Correspondingly, through *this* unprecedented Consciousness *Transformation,* there is Unveiled and Revealed the full and complete *Recognition* (transcendence but inclusion) of the shadow vestiges of the polarity-duality-base illusion of separate (and separate-self-sense) *subject-versus-object* consciousness. Consequently, and correspondingly, there now emerges and occurs One's *full* and *complete Recognition* (transcendence but inclusion) of polarity-duality's separate *subject-versus-object based* shadow vestiges of *pre-personal, personal-egoic* and *conditioned social-cultural* compound self realities of mind consciousness. Now, without such polarity-duality-based separate *subject-versus-object* consciousness, upon which compound personal-egoic self realities of consciousness are founded and established, these three contingent and relative compound personal-egoic self realities have neither the *grounding* of structure nor function to operate, and thus they no longer *at all* arise or occur in Recognition Consciousness.

One's full and complete transcendent *Revelation* and *Recognition*, but not as yet either partial or complete transcendent *Realization*, of unconditioned and uncontracted Nondual Self-as-Self Wisdom and Compassion Consciousness occurs at the developmental *culmination* of realm-wave *primordial* Causal Arch-istent Holistence. Thus, it is this Luminous Transformative and Transfigurative Nondual Self-as-Self *Recognition Enlightenment* within *primordial* Causal Arch-istent Holistence Consciousness that marks this realm-wave's termination, and, in turn, *precipitates* the holon-only realm-wave of *primordial* Causal Omni-istent Holistence Consciousness (see Figures 2, 3, 4, 6 and 7).

Partial *Realization* of Nondual Self-as-Self within Causal Omni-istence Consciousness

The realm-wave emergence of holon-only *primordial* Causal Omni-istent Holistence Consciousness is marked by One's *initial* and *preliminary* (partial) developmental transcendent *Realization* of the Onliness and Ultimacy that is Nondual Self of no-self Enlightenment Awakening, this Bliss-Devine transcendental Remembrance of *trans-mental* and *trans-egoic* Wisdom, Communion and Compassion Self Reality. However, within One's developmental unfolding of the *initial* sub-realm-wave of *primordial* Causal Omni-istence there is Revealed only a *partial* and *incomplete* transcendent *Realization of,* and *Identity with,* Self of Nondual Spirit-as-Spirit Consciousness.

Thus, within *primordial* Causal Omni-istence there is Revealed a yet more Consciousness Inclusive, but still partial and incomplete, transcendence but inclusion *Realization* of the illusion of One's unmanifest shadow vestige of polarity-within-unity and duality Consciousness. However, through *partial* and *incomplete* transcendence of this polarity-duality Consciousness *illusion*, there also necessarily occurs a partially and incompletely *Realized* transcendence but inclusion of One's related shadow vestiges of polarity-duality's separate *subject-versus-object* consciousness. And through this, there necessarily and correspondingly occurs a *partial* and *incomplete* transcendence but inclusion transpersonal Realization of polarity-duality's separate *subject-versus-object based* shadow vestiges of *pre-personal, personal-egoic* and *conditioned social-cultural* compound self realities of mind and consciousness. Recall, that with only partial and incomplete polarity-duality-based separate *subject-object* consciousness, these contingent and relative compound personal-egoic self realities have only a partial and incomplete structural and functional grounding, have only a limited basis on which to be established and operate, and thus can only partially and incompletely arise and occur in such Realization Consciousness.

Fully *Realized* Nondual Self-as-Self within Causal Trans-omni-istence Consciousness

One's transcendent developmental Consciousness within holon-only *primordial* Causal Omni-istent Holistence *culminates* in the unprecedented *full* and *complete Recognition, Remembrance* and *Realization* (thus Recognition-only transcendence but inclusion *within* Realization) of Bliss-Divine Nondual Self-as-Self Truth-consciousness Reality. In Onliness theory, this is the *final* holonic (including *both* holon-polarity-within-unity and holon-only) realm-wave of *all* realm-wave developmental-evolutionary Consciousness.

It is One's developmental emergence within sub-realm-wave *primordial* Causal Trans-omni-istence Consciousness that, at its culmination, is marked by the *full* and *complete* trans-rational and trans-mental Realization and Remembrance *of,* and Identity *with,* Nondual Spirit-as-Spirit Self of Perfect Emptiness and Fullness. Thus, at this realm-wave's culmination, there is *fully* and *completely* Revealed this *Trans-pre-personal, Transpersonal-transegoic, Trans-conditioned-social-cultural,* and *Trans-perspectival* Nondual Self-as-Self Consciousness Reality, that You and I always already are, have ever been and will ever be. And with this Awakened transcendent *Realization*, there is, for the first time, *transcendence but inclusion,* negation and preservation, of *all* holonic (holon-polaric and holon-only) realm-wave worldspace Realities of Consciousness (see Figures 2, 3, 4, 6 and 7).

This *ultimate* transcendent Consciousness Remembrance and Realization of *uncreated* and *timeless* Nondual Self-as-Self Reality marks the developmental completion of One's *final* holon-only *primordial* Causal Omni-istent Holistence realm-wave, (and, indeed, the developmental completion of One's broader holon-only realm-wave of the unmanifest, formless, and boundless Consciousness that is Recognized and Realized within Causal Holistence Reality Itself). There now occurs the *full* Realization that

You are *All* and *Only* Universal Spirit. In Onliness theory then, *this* is the Nondual Spirit-as-Spirit *Remembrance* and *Realization Enlightenment* of holon-only *primordial* Causal Omni-istent Holistence Consciousness. And, in turn, it is this transcendent Nondual Bliss-Divine Self *Realization,* at the culmination of Causal Holistence Consciousness, that *precipitates* emergence of the *Absolute* and *Infinite* Enlightenment of T*rans-holonic* and *Trans-realm-wave* Nondual Spirit-as-Spirit Consciousness Awakening Itself (see Figures 2, 3, 4, 6 and 7).

With One's *Supreme* Nondual Truth-consciousness Awakening, there occurs *full* and *complete Realization* (transcendence, but inclusion within such transcendence) of *all* remaining unmanifest shadow vestige illusions of separate *subject-versus-object* polaric consciousness. That is to say, there now occurs, and is *fully Revealed,* the complete transcendence-but-inclusion *Realization* of polarity-duality's separate *subject-object based* contingent shadow vestiges of separate-self-sense *pre-personal-pre-egoic, personal-egoic,* and *conditioned social-cultural* compound self realities of mind and consciousness. With such *Supreme* Truth-consciousness Awakening, then, One's relative and singular-perspective based compound personal-egoic self realities of consciousness have no foundational structural and functional basis of establishment and operation, and thus can no longer at all arise or occur in Consciousness.

In this way, there now occurs the *final death* of these *ultimately illusory* separate *subject-object based* narcissistic vestige shadows of pre-personal, personal-egoic, and conditioned social-cultural compound self realities of mind and consciousness. And thus, the enabled *Birth Awakening* of *Trans-perspectival, Trans-relative, Trans-conditioned* and *Trans-conditional* Nondual Self-as-Self Consciousness Enlightenment; which is this ultimately *Unqualifable* and *Unspeakable* Awakened Self of *Freedom* and *Responsibility* Complete.

With this final and complete *transcendence* (but inclusion within such transcendence) of realm-wave Causal Holistence Consciousness, You *fully* Realize that no vestige of polaric-based separate-self-sense "I-me-mine-ness" illusion remains *of* or *about* You. Kosmic Awakened Nondual Self Reality and Consciousness *is* Your *complete* and *only* Nature, Identity and Condition. As Nondual Self-as-Self Awakened Consciousness, You are only and none other than this *Am*, of and as All, Each and Every organic and non-organic Being and Entity of Consciousness. In Truth-consciousness, You are the *Absolute Reality* of All and of None, and of Neither.

One's Nondual Consciousness Transition from Temporary State to Permanent Trait

This *culmination* of Universal Spirit's Causal Holistence Consciousness is also marked by the transition *from* One's predominantly transient *temporary state* transcendent Awareness and Experience of Awakened Nondual Consciousness Realization, *to* an ongoing, stable, and predominantly continuous *permanent trait* transcendent Awakened *Self* of Nondual Consciousness Reality. And it is this developmental-evolutionary emergence of such a *permanent trait onset* that plays a *critical* role in marking One's *initial* transition into Nondual Spirit-as-Spirit Awakened Consciousness Itself.

With the full Awakening to, and complete Remembrance and Realization of, this Bliss-Devine Nondual Self-as-Self Reality that You *truly* are, You *Return* to Where You always, already have *ever* Been, and will *ever* Be. That is, You Return to this "Worldspace" of *all* Consciousness worldspaces, which *is* Mind of Nondual Spirit-as-Spirit Self Reality (which Itself is and is not a Worldspace, and is neither). Also, this Bliss-Divine Self Reality that You always already are, is *neither* a separate *holon-only* realm-wave (as in Universal Spirit's Causal Holistence Consciousness) or a *holon-polar* realm-wave (as in World Soul's Psychic Multi-istence and Subtle Prim-istence Consciousness), *nor* is It not. Beloved, moment-to-moment, simply Live *As*, *Out of*, and *Through* this Awakened Beauty, Truth and Goodness of *Supreme Self* that You are, and have ever been. Mindfully, with loving kindness, equanimity and humility, simply *Be* this Luminous God-conscious Self of *Power* and *Vision*, that is Your *true* Nature, Identity and Condition (see Figures 2, 3, 4, 5, 6 and 7).

Awakened Self of Nondual Consciousness Reality At Once *Is* and *Is-not* Knowable

Self of *Trans-manifest* and *Trans-ist* Nondual Consciousness Realization is the *all-inclusive* Ground, Goal and Source *of* and *from* which all Consciousness holon-polar and holon-only realm-waves arise, and to which they *all* return. Such Nondual Self-as-Self Remembrance is radically *Trans-perspectival, Trans-holonic, Trans-pre-personal-pre-egoic, Trans-personal-egoic, Trans-conditioned-social-cultural, Trans-polaric* (and thus *Trans-separate-subject-object*), *Trans-perspectival* and *Trans-realm-wave* Consciousness Realization. Ultimately, however, such Awakened Nondual Self Realization transcends but includes, It *both is and is-not, and is neither*, all of these dimensions of Consciousness. Witness-and-that-which-is-witnessed is no longer two, nor is It one.

You Are this All-Consciousness Inclusive Self Reality of Truth and Loving Kindness

In each of the previously discussed seven diagrams, this Bliss-Devine *Self* of Nondual Spirit-as-Spirit Consciousness that You *actually* are, is *symbolized* by *all* that is written and blank, by the paper substance, ink, as well as all perceived surfaces and ink-marked images and words (see Figures 1 through 7). This ultimately *unfathomable* and *unknowable* Awakened Nondual Self-as-Self Reality Expresses and Embraces all *Ascent* (which is the highest Ascent) of *transcendent* Wisdom (Eros), and all *Descent* (which is the deepest Descent) of *immanent* Compassion (Agape) for *each* and *every* Consciousness Being and Entity, and thus for *all* of Reality. *This* is the All-Consciousness Inclusive, Embracing and Encompassing *Self Reality* that You *truly* and *completely* are, of infinite and boundless *Wisdom* and *Loving Kindness*.

Unmediated and Direct Comprehension Is At the Heart of Wisdom and Compassion

Because holon-polarity-within-unity's separate-self-sense

subject-versus-object based *singular perspective* pre-personal, personal-egoic and conditioned social-cultural compound self realities of mind *no longer* arise or occur (are *transcended* but included) within Self of Nondual Consciousness, One's All-inclusive *Intuitive* Insight, Comprehension and Knowledge are now *unmediated* and *direct*. In this way, such Intuitive Insight, Comprehension and Knowledge are trans-mentally *beyond* mediated-indirect, interpreted, co-constructed and co-created *polaric* separate subject-versus-object *mental* (mind) interpretation. And so it is this Trans-perspectival, Trans-conditional, Trans-pre-personal, Trans-conditioned-social-cultural and Trans-personal-egoic direct, immediate and complete *Intuitive Comprehension* that is the *Opening*, *Ground* and *Source* of One's *Supreme Self* Awakened and Realized Wisdom and Compassion.

Only Brahman, Only Christ-consciousness Is, and You are *That* and non-other Than

Beloved, *You* are this *Luminous Mind* of Wisdom and Compassion Consciousness, here and now. You are *always* and *already* this Awakened Self of Nondual Bliss-Devine Enlightenment *only*, without a second. There is *only* Brahman, *only* Christ-consciousness, and You are *That* and non-other Than. *You* are *This Radiance* of uncreated and timeless Nondual Self-as-Self Reality.

Realize and Confess that You Are the Very Godhead of God-consciousness Itself

This *Trans-ist* Nondual Spirit-as-Spirit Awakened Realization that You are right now, is *fully* and *completely* Trans-polaric, Trans-holonic, Trans-realm-wave, Trans-conditioned-social-cultural, Trans-personal-egoic, Trans-pre-personal, Trans-mental, Trans-rational, Trans-perspectival, and Trans-conditional (beyond relative conditions and circumstances). This *All* and *None* and *Neither* Identity and Condition of Nondual no-self Self *Krishna-consciousness* and *Buddha-mind,* that You *ever* are, includes and embraces (and also transcends) *both* the Many and the

One, Form and Emptiness, Nirvana and Samsara, Polarity-Duality and Non-polarity-Non-duality. Beloved, *Realize* and *Confess* that You *are* Brahman-Atman, the very *Godhead* of God-consciousness Itself, and *none other* Than.

In Onliness theory and perspective, One who fully *Realizes* Nondual Self Awakened Consciousness will nonetheless, as yet a *manifest* embodied Being or Entity, continue to develop-evolve within One's particular *manifest* embodiment expression of this ever changing and evolving Form Reality. However, such development-evolution will occur in Ways that predominantly *transcend but include* the ways of Beings who have *not yet* fully Realized transcendent Nondual Enlightenment Awakening.

For One who has fully *Awakened to* and *Realizes* Bliss-Devine Nondual Self-as-Self Reality, such *continuing* development-evolution will, in Onliness theory and perspective, occur in both One's *pre-transcendental consciousness* form embodiment, within physical body, mind, emotion, and social-cultural developmental consciousness, as well as in One's *transcendental* Consciousness form embodiment, within World Soul and Universal Spirit realm-wave developmental Consciousness. But *this* development-evolution will occur *within* and *through* Choiceless, Unconditioned, and Uncontracted *Actlessness,* which will *transcend* (but include from the *Vision* of such transcendence) the *ordeal* of samsaric willful action, struggle, suffering and turmoil.

Nothing Special and Apart. Just This

Always keep in mind, that this *Absolute Self* of Nondual Awakened transcendent Consciousness Realization is *not* outwardly conspicuous, but rather is *humble, ordinary* and *everyday,* and that such Realization is certainly not achievable or possessable, but, rather, is always already Your and My *true* Nature and Condition - *infinitely, eternally* and *unconditionally.* But again, due to our samsaric delusion, blindness and ignorance, we do not *Recognize* the birthless and deathless Nature and Condition of this Bliss-Devine Self Reality that We *timelessly* and *inherently* are.

That is to say, this *Radiant Abyss Self* of Everything and Nothing - of *All* and *None,* this Luminous *Emptiness* and *Silence* of ultimate *Freedom* and *Liberation,* that We *ever* are. But ordinary, *nothing* special and apart. *Just This.*

"A knower of Brahman becomes Brahman." This Mind of Fire

Beloved, *Know* and *Confess* that You are this unqualifiable Self of *Supreme Identity*, this Awakened Spirit-as-Spirit Enlightenment *only*, without an opposite. You are this transcendent *Mind of Fire*. The *Upanishads* put it well: "A knower of Brahman becomes Brahman."

You are Unconditioned and Uncreated Suchness, this Is-ness Mind of Consciousness

This *Absolute Consciousness* Reality of *Self* that You always, already are, which is Your *True* Identity, Nature and Condition, indeed *is* Godhead, *is* God, utterly, only and completely. But understand, You are *not* this *myth* of an all-powerful God, that, as compound personal-egoic consciousness and self of mind, you conceive and speak of in *dualistic* terms, as some kind of *separate* and *external* God, who is somehow in charge of manipulating and controlling *separate* other-ness, other Beings and Entities that are *separate from* this mythic *illusionary* God. You *are*, and indeed *each* and *every* Consciousness Being and Entity *is*, this transcendent *Nondual Self* of no-self, which is the very *Consciousness of God.*

Again, and finally, from Onliness perspective, Awakened Nondual Spirit-as-Spirit Realization *is* this Self of unknowable, radiant and eternal *Emptiness*. And You *are* this unconditioned and uncreated *Suchness*, this Is-ness *Mind* of Intuitive Trans-perspectival and Trans-conditional Consciousness. You are *already* Buddha, and thus Buddha-nature Itself. You are Self's *Realization* as Atman-Brahman, Christ-consciousness, God-consciousness. *Remember* and *Confess* that You are always already Nondual Self-as-Self Awakened Consciousness, but *not* as your predominant-exclusive polarity-duality-based separate-self-sense pre-personal-pre-egoic, personal-egoic, and conditioned social-cultural compound self reality of mind and consciousness alone.

Choicelessly, in Actlessness, You are Always Already Pure Spirit In Every Moment

In Reality, You *are* this *Onliness* of Self and Self *Only,* this unborn and undying *Am* of Buddha-mind Enlightenment. Choicelessly, in *Actlessness*, You neither come nor go, yet are always already Pure Spirit, unqualifable *Godhead*, in each and every moment. Far beyond words, ideas, images and conceptions, *You* are this ever-present *Radiance* of Nondual Self-as-Self *Awakened* Consciousness Reality, this Permanent Presence, embracing Each and All - each-where, all-where, every-where, nowhere, now-here. Beloved, You *are* this transcendent *uncontracted* Self of *Mystery,* Openly and Freely arising, emerging, Ascending-Descending, as the *entire* radiant Kosmos and Beyond - infinitely, causelessly boundlessly, timelessly.

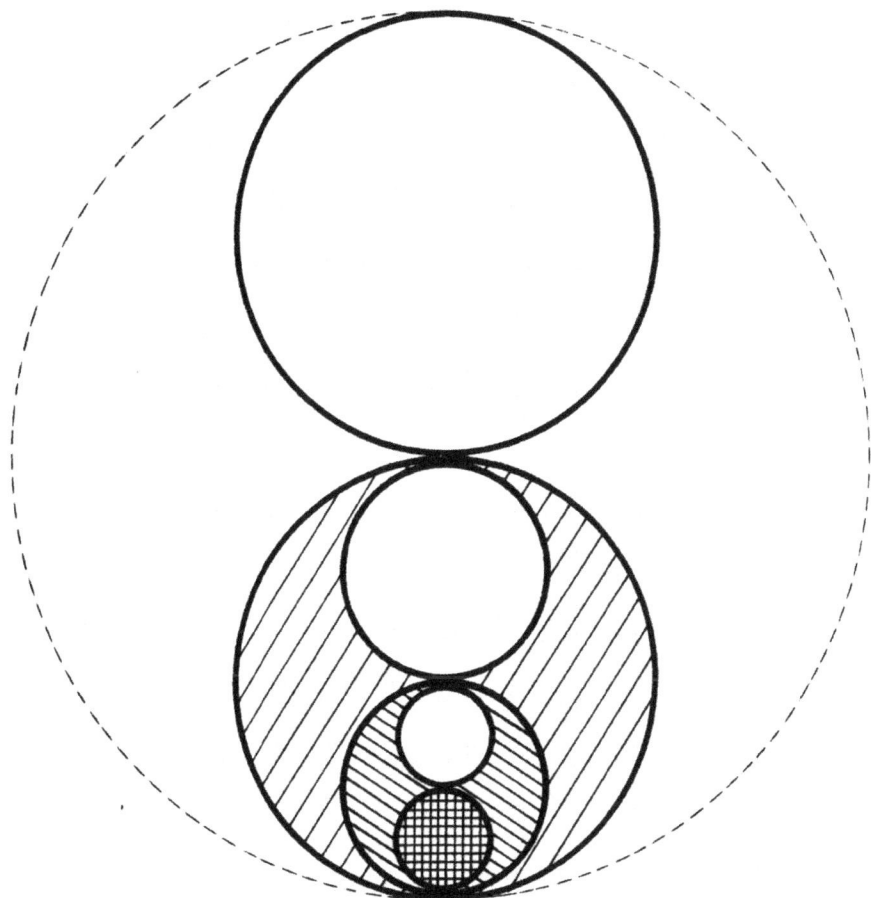

FIGURE 1

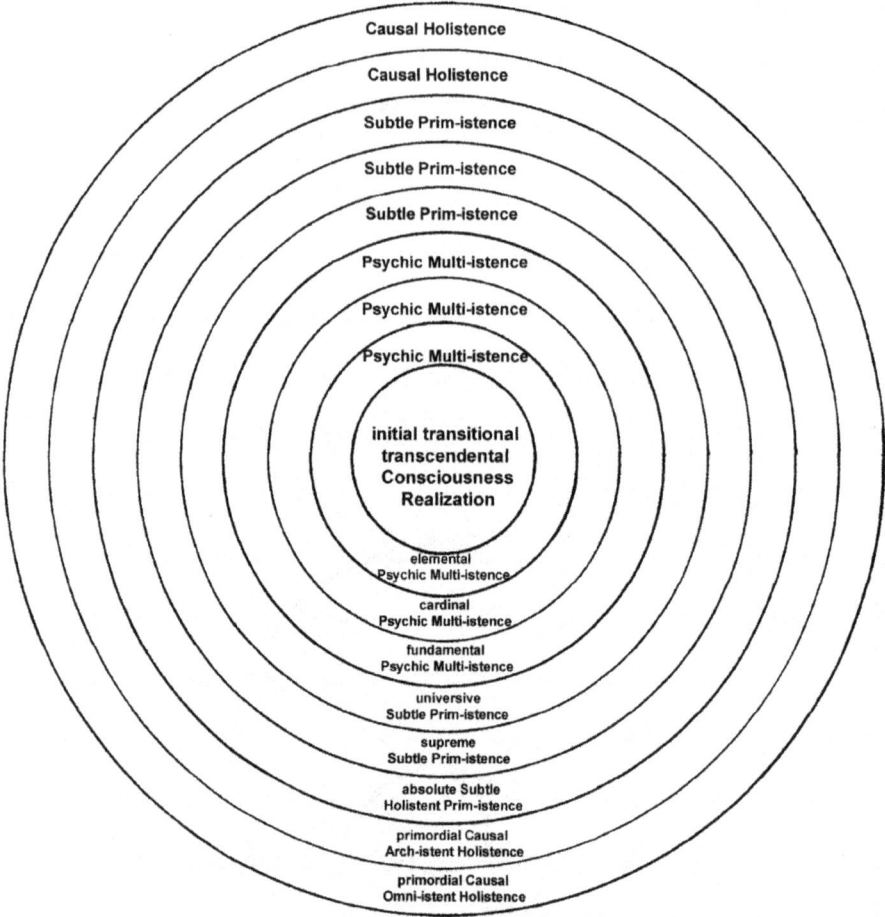

Causal Holistence

Causal Holistence

Subtle Prim-istence

Subtle Prim-istence

Subtle Prim-istence

Psychic Multi-istence

Psychic Multi-istence

Psychic Multi-istence

initial transitional
transcendental
Consciousness
Realization

elemental
Psychic Multi-istence

cardinal
Psychic Multi-istence

fundamental
Psychic Multi-istence

universive
Subtle Prim-istence

supreme
Subtle Prim-istence

absolute Subtle
Holistent Prim-istence

primordial Causal
Arch-istent Holistence

primordial Causal
Omni-istent Holistence

Holonic-concept diagram (i.e., holon-only versus integrated holon-polar diagram) of the developmental-evolutionary Ascent-Descent of transcendental Consciousness in Onliness theory and perspective.

FIGURE 2

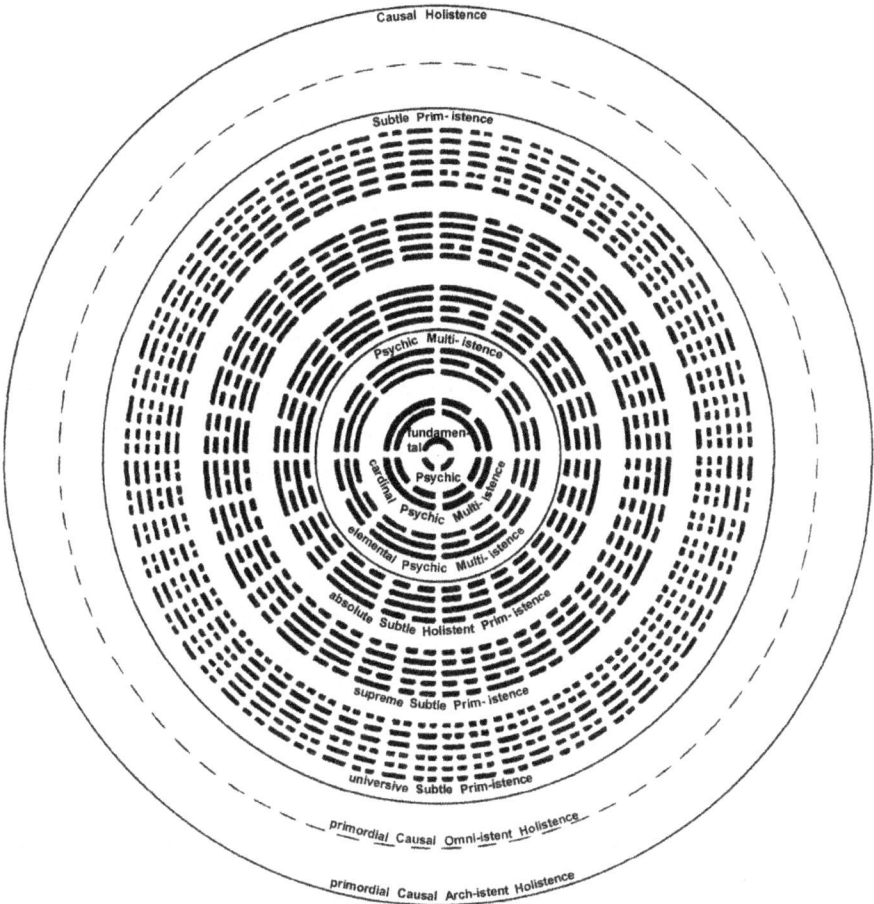

Causal Holistence

Subtle Prim-istence

Psychic Multi-istence

Fundamental Psychic

cardinal Psychic Multi-istence

elemental Psychic Multi-istence

absolute Subtle Holistent Prim-istence

supreme Subtle Prim-istence

universe Subtle Prim-istence

primordial Causal Omni-istent Holistence

primordial Causal Arch-istent Holistence

FIGURE 3

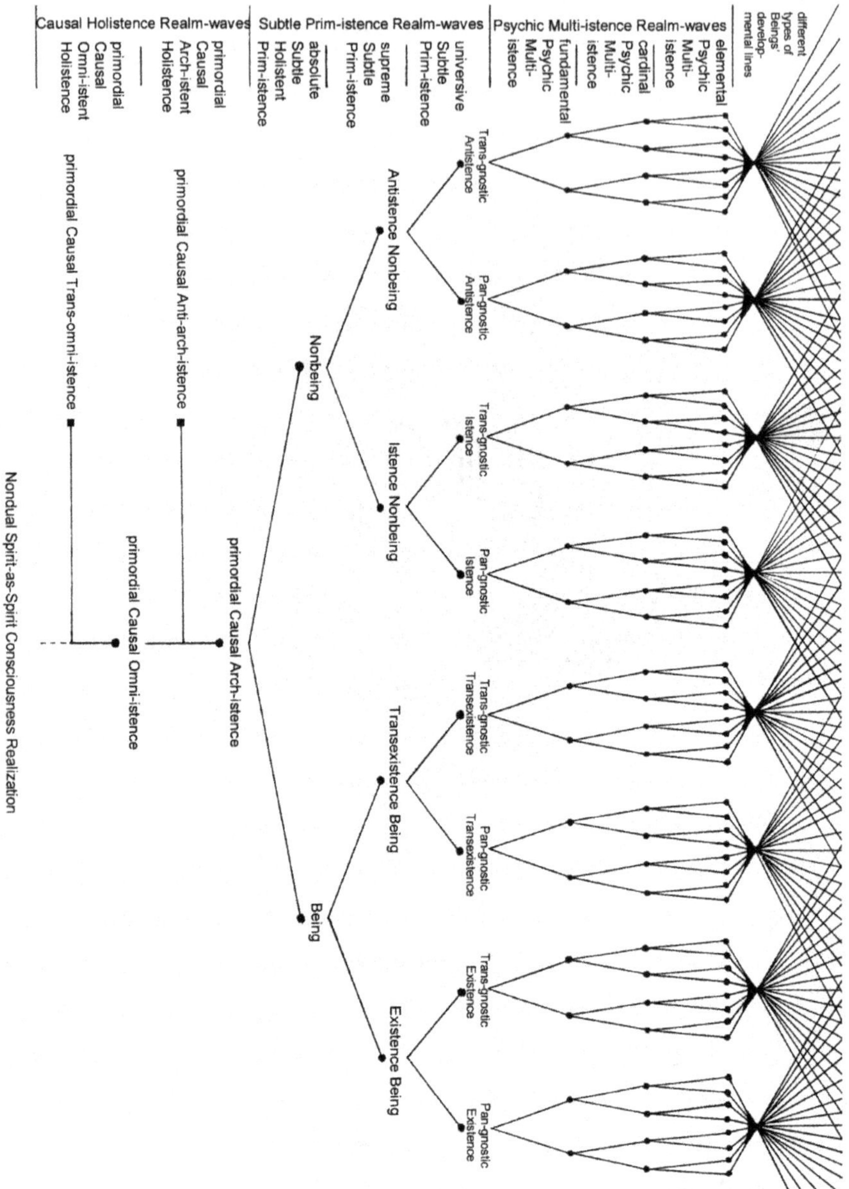
different types of Beings' develop-mental lines
Psychic Multi-istence Realm-waves
elemental Psychic Multi-istence
cardinal Psychic Multi-istence
fundamental Psychic Multi-istence
Subtle Prim-istence Realm-waves
universive Subtle Prim-istence
supreme Subtle Prim-istence
absolute Subtle Holistent Prim-istence
Causal Holistence Realm-waves
primordial Causal Arch-istent Holistence
primordial Causal Omni-istent Holistence
Trans-gnostic Antistence
Pan-gnostic Antistence
Trans-gnostic Istence
Pan-gnostic Istence
Trans-gnostic Transexistence
Pan-gnostic Transexistence
Trans-gnostic Existence
Pan-gnostic Existence
Antistence Nonbeing
Istence Nonbeing
Transexistence Being
Existence Being
Nonbeing
Being
primordial Causal Anti-arch-istence
primordial Causal Trans-omni-istence
primordial Causal Arch-istence
primordial Causal Omni-istence
Nondual Spirit-as-Spirit Consciousness Realization

FIGURE 4

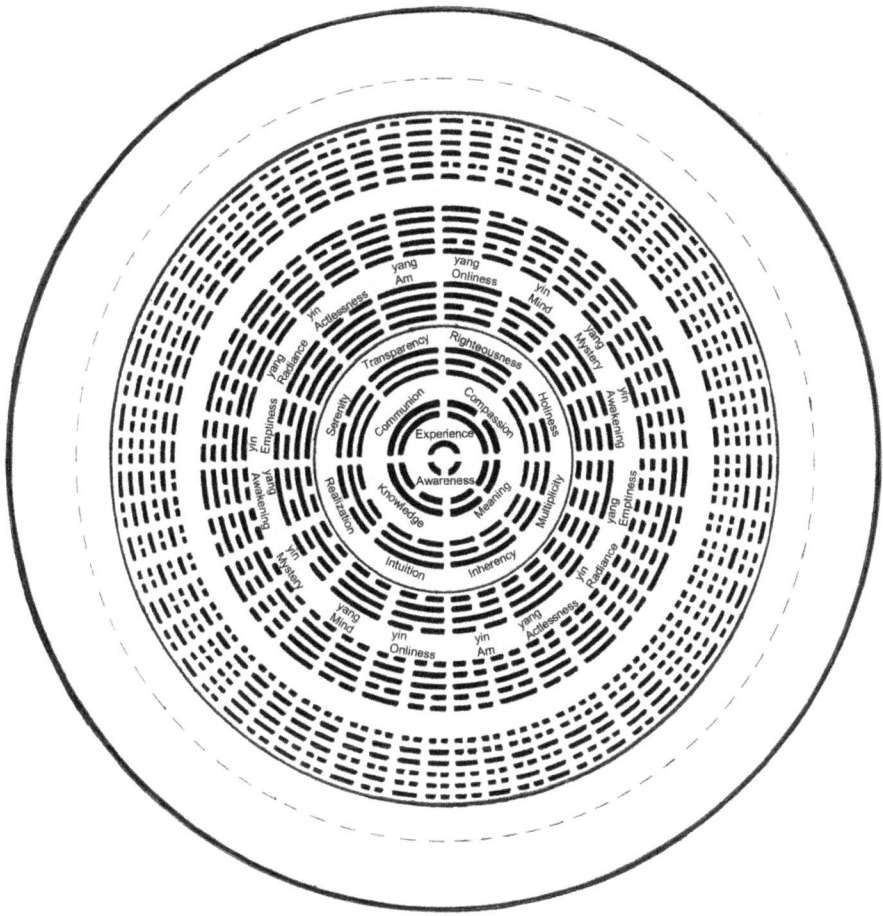

FIGURE 5

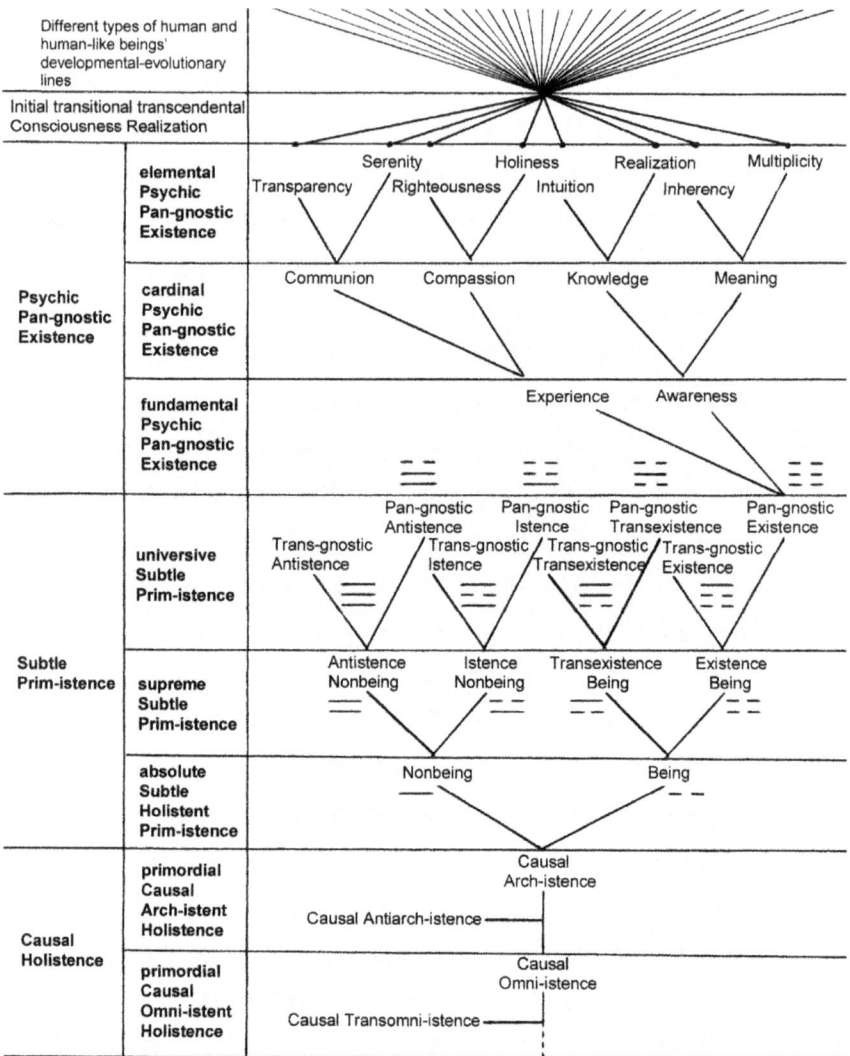

FIGURE 6

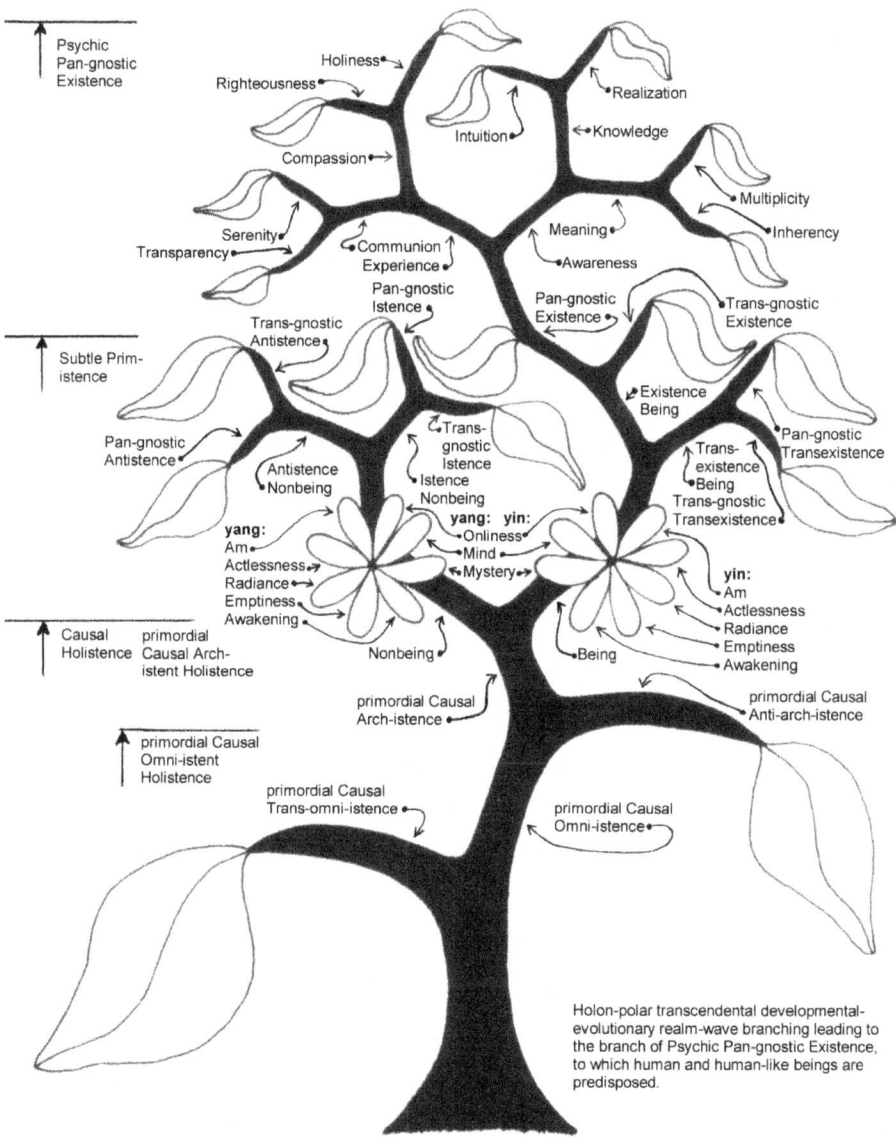

Psychic
Pan-gnostic
Existence

Holiness
Righteousness
Realization
Intuition
Knowledge
Compassion
Multiplicity
Serenity
Inherency
Transparency
Communion
Experience
Meaning
Pan-gnostic
Istence
Awareness
Pan-gnostic
Existence
Trans-gnostic
Existence

Subtle Prim-
istence

Trans-gnostic
Antistence
Existence
Being
Pan-gnostic
Antistence
Pan-gnostic
Transexistence
Antistence
Nonbeing
Trans-
gnostic
Istence
Istence
Nonbeing
Trans-
existence
Being
Trans-gnostic
Transexistence

yang:
Am
Actlessness
Radiance
Emptiness
Awakening

yang: yin:
Onliness
Mind
Mystery

yin:
Am
Actlessness
Radiance
Emptiness
Awakening

Nonbeing

Being

Causal   primordial
Holistence Causal Arch-
           istent Holistence

primordial Causal
Arch-istence

primordial Causal
Anti-arch-istence

primordial Causal
Omni-istent
Holistence

primordial Causal
Trans-omni-istence

primordial Causal
Omni-istence

Holon-polar transcendental developmental-
evolutionary realm-wave branching leading to
the branch of Psychic Pan-gnostic Existence,
to which human and human-like beings are
predisposed.

FIGURE 7

Enlightenment's Awakening | 113

References

Adi Da Samraj (Da Free John) (1985). *The Dawn Horse Testament of Heart-Master Da Free John*. Middletown, CA: The Dawn Horse Press.

Adi Da Samraj (1995). *The Knee of Listening: The Early-Life Ordeal and the Radical Spiritual Realization of the Divine World-Teacher*. Middletown, CA: The Dawn Horse Press.

Blofeld, J. (Translator and Editor) (1968). *I Ching: The Book of Change*. New York: E. P. Dutton and Co.

Feng, G. and J. English (Translators) (1972). *Lao Tsu: Tao Te Ching*. New York: Vintage Books.

Huxley, A. (1944). *The Perennial Philosophy*. New York: Harper & Row.

Isherwood, C. (Editor) (1972). *Vedanta for Modern Man*. New York: The New American Library, Inc.

Kapleau, P. (Compiler) (1965). *The Three Pillars of Zen: Teaching Practice Enlightenment*. Boston: Beacon Press.

King James Version. *The Holy Bible*. New York: World Publishing Co.

Lama Surya Das (1997). *Awakening the Buddha Within*. New York: Broadway Books-Bantam Doubleday Dell Publishing Group, Inc.

Lau, D. C. (Translator) (1988). *Lao Tzu: Tao Te Ching*. New York: Penguin Books.

Legge, J. (Translator and Editor) (1964). *I Ching: Book of Changes*. New York: Bantam Books, Inc.

Meyer, M. (Translator) (1984). *The Secret Teaching of Jesus: Four Gnostic Gospels.* New York: Vintage Books.

Mitchell, S. (Compiler) (1991). *The Enlightened Mind: An Anthology of Sacred Prose.* New York: Harper.

Mitchell, S. (Translator) (1991). *Tao Te Ching: A New English Version.* New York: HarperCollins Publishers.

Reps, P. (Compiler) (1989). *Zen Flesh, Zen Bones: A Collection of Zen and pre-Zen Writings.* New York: Anchor Book-Doubleday.

Ross, N. (Compiler and Editor) (1960). *The World of Zen: An East-West Anthology.* New York: Vintage Books.

Sri Aurobindo (Compiled by P. B. Saint-Hilaire) (1995). *The Future Evolution of Man: The Divine Life upon Earth.* Pondicherry, India: Sri Aurobindo Ashram Publication Department.

Sri Nisargadatta Maharaj (Translated by M. Frydman) (2012). *I Am That: Talks with Sri Nisargadatta Maharaj.* Durham, North Carolina: The Acorn Press.

Sri Ramana Maharshi (Translated by T. M. P. Mahadevan) (2008). *Who Am I: The Teachings of Bhagavan Sri Ramana Maharshi.* Tiruvannamal   606 603 Tamil Nadu, India: V. S. Ramanan, President, Board of Trustees Sri Ramanasramam.

Suzuki. D. T. (Compiler) (1960). *Manual of Zen Buddhism.* New York: Grove Press, Inc.

Swami Prabhavananda and F. Manchester (Translators and Editors) (1957). *The Upanishads: Breath of the Eternal.* New York: The New American Library-Mentor Books.

Swami Prabhavananda and C. Isherwood (Translators) (1960). *The Song of God: Bhagavad-Gita.* New York: The New American Library-Mentor Books.

Treon, M. (1981a). "Organismic communicology: a prologue - dead leaves and living shadows moving in the wind." *Papers In Linguistics: International Journal of Human Communication,* 14 (1), 131-148.

Treon, M. (1981b). "Organismic communicology: a second prologue - reflection, shadow and illusion." *Papers In Linguistics: International Journal of Human Communication, 14 (3), 359-375.*

Treon, M. (1989). *The Tao of Onliness: An I Ching Cosmology - The Awakening Years.* Santa Barbara, CA: Fithian Press.

Treon, M. (1996). *Fires of Consciousness: The Tao of Onliness I Ching.* Goodyear, AZ: Auroral Skies Press.

Treon, M. (2009). *Uncreated Timeless Self of Radiant Emptiness - Onliness Consciousness and Commentaries: Formulations of a Post-metaphysical Integral Transpersonal Communicology.* Goodyear, AZ: Auroral Skies Press.

Treon, M. (2011). *Enlightenment Dialogues: A Journey of Post-metaphysical Onliness Awakening.* Goodyear, AZ: Auroral Skies Press.

Wilber, K. (1980). *The Atman Project: A Transpersonal View of Human Development.* Wheaton, IL: Quest.

Wilber, K. (1981). *Up From Eden: A Transpersonal View of Human Evolution.* New York: Doubleday-Anchor.

Wilber, K. (1983). *Eye to Eye: The Quest for the New Paradigm.* Boston: Shambhala Publications.

Wilber, K. (1984). *A Sociable God: Toward a New Understanding of Religion.* Boston: Shambhala Publications.

Wilber, K. (1995). *Sex, Ecology, Spirituality: The Spirit of Evolution.* Boston: Shambhala Publications.

Wilber, K. (1996). *A Brief History of Everything.* Boston: Shambhala Publications.

Wilber, K. (1997). *The Eye of Spirit: An Integral Vision for a World Gone Slightly Mad.* Boston: Shambhala Publications.

Wilber, K. (1998). *The Marriage of Sense and Soul: Integrating Science and Religion.* New York: Random House, Inc.

Wilber, K. (2000). *One Taste: The Journals of Ken Wilber.* Boston: Shambhala Publications.

Wilber, K. (1999-2000). *The Collected Works of Ken Wilber,* Vol. 1-8. Boston: Shambhala Publications.

Wilber, K. (1999-2000, vol. 4). *Integral Psychology: Consciousness, Spirit, Psychology, Therapy.* (in *The Collected Works of Ken Wilber,* vol. 4). Boston: Shambhala Publications.

Wilber, K. (2004). *The Simple Feeling of Being: Embracing Your True Nature.* Boston: Shambhala Publications.

Wilber, K. (2007). *Integral Spirituality: A Startling New Role for Religion in the Modern and Postmodern World.* Boston: Integral Books-Shambhala Publications.

Wilber, K., J. Engler and D. P. Brown (1986). *Transformations of Consciousness: Conventional and Contemplative Perspectives on Development.* Boston: Shambhala Publications.

www.ingramcontent.com/pod-product-compliance
Lightning Source LLC
Chambersburg PA
CBHW061735020426

42331CB00006B/1248

9 780965 574051